HOW TO
WRITE A STORY

HOW TO WRITE A STORY

BY KATHLEEN C. PHILLIPS

A SPEAK OUT, WRITE ON! BOOK
Franklin Watts
New York / Chicago / London / Sydney

Excerpts from *Hailstones and Halibut Bones*, by Mary O'Neill and Leonard Weisgard III. Copyright © 1961 by Mary LeDuc O'Neill. Used by permission of Doubleday, a division of Bantam Doubleday Dell Publishing Group, Inc.
Excerpts from "Zero Weather," *Runny Days, Sunny Days*, by Aileen Fisher. Copyright © 1958 by Aileen Fisher. Used by permission of the author.

Library of Congress Cataloging-in-Publication Data

Phillips, Kathleen C.
How to write a story / Kathleen C. Phillips.
p. cm.— (Speak out, write on!)
Includes bibliographical references and index.
Summary: Examines the basics of writing a story, from finding a title and beginning the work to completing and revising it.
ISBN 0-531-11239-X
1. Authorship—Juvenile literature. [1. Authorship. 2. Creative writing.] I. Title. II. Series: Speak out, write on! book.
PN159.P55   1995
808.3—dc20   95-2073
                                                                       CIP AC

For Jane Fitz-Randolph
and Brad Phillips,
with appreciation

ONTENTS

HOW TO
WRITE A STORY

*I*NTRODUCTION: TO BEGIN WITH

To begin with, why write? Writing is rather like talking to yourself. Writing gives an opportunity to remember, to relive, and to rethink experiences, and it helps to give perspective and shape to your own thoughts and ideas. Writing is a way of getting acquainted with yourself.

Why write for others? Writing is communication. It is moving a thought from one mind, yours, to another mind, your reader's. In all the world, in all of time, there is only one you. Only you see the world through your eyes, your experiences, your imagination. Writing creatively is not necessarily saying something that has never been said before in a way that has never been said before. Writing creatively is saying something so that your readers will see in a way they have never seen before. Whether you have thought about it or not, you, from the perspective and viewpoint that is yours alone, have something to say, something to share with others.

Why read books on writing? One of the oldest clichés about writing is that it is a talent that can't be taught. True, talent can't be taught . . . but Ralph

Waldo Emerson pointed out that talent alone cannot make a writer. Becoming a writer is a journey of writing, of trial and error, and writing again.

Travelers going to unfamiliar places use maps prepared by those who have gone before. Books about writing are the charts and guideposts that experienced writers prepare to make easier journeys for the inexperienced, and to help good writers become better writers.

To quote novelist Phyllis A. Whitney, "No one can light in you the spark that will make you a writer, make you want to write. You must supply that yourself."[1] But if you have the spark, you will find many people, through books and magazines, classes and workshops, who are eager to help you fan that spark into a lively flame.

ONE

BUILDING HOUSES AND CREATING STORIES

Remember those house builders, the Three Little Pigs? And remember that demolition expert, the Big, Bad Wolf?

The first two Little Pigs were in such a hurry to go off and do other things that they built their houses too quickly and too carelessly. The Third Little Pig built a house of sturdy bricks instead of sticks or straw, and he put it together with care. The houses of sticks and straw tumbled down when the Wolf huffed and puffed, but the carefully built house stood strong.

Have you ever thought about the ways good stories and good houses are alike?

The careful house builder starts out with a solid foundation, then puts up a strong framework that can support the walls and roof, and, last, adds doors and window glass, paint and trim.

The storyteller needs to build a foundation and framework that is dependable enough to support the details of a story.

A story and a house might be compared this way:

Idea = Foundation
Story plan or plot = Framework
Details of story = Walls and roof
Ways of telling the story = Floors and doors
Windows, paint, and trim

BUILDING PLANS

The builder follows a plan, one step at a time. If the builder tries to put up a framework without the foundation first, or a roof without the framework first, the house will fall apart.

For similar reasons, storytellers need plans. Their plans are not as detailed and complicated as builders' plans, but by following a few simple steps as they work, storytellers can keep their stories from falling apart.

The builder's working directions are scale drawings and lists of specifications—the requirements to follow and the materials to use.

Our storytelling directions include a short plan for making a story framework and a list of questions to help in working out details. But first comes the foundation.

IDEA = FOUNDATION

Where do ideas for stories come from? The answer to that question is

EVERYWHERE!

Ideas are all around us, so the first steps in finding them are learning to recognize them and then remembering to catch them.

Are you a people watcher? Do you like to roam the malls or sit in airports and look at the people going by? Watch how they walk, listen to how they talk and to what they say? Do you notice what they wear, wonder about their jobs, imagine their family life?

Where else, besides by watching and listening to people, can you find ideas? They are there in the movies and television programs you watch, in the music you listen to, in what you read, and in your memories and your day-to-day experiences.

You'll find ideas in your travels away from home and in your own neighborhood, in high occasions and in your everyday life.

You can find ideas in almost everything you read, and sometimes those ideas come quite unexpectedly. Something you read reminds you of a person, a happening, an experience, and it starts you on a new train of thought. This doesn't mean that you are taking someone else's idea to use and call your own, it means that someone else's idea, considered through your experience and your perspective, can inspire a new idea that is your own.

Many writers carry pocket-size notebooks with them in order to jot down entries, because they've learned that note making has two benefits. First, the most wonderful idea in the world will be of no use if it's forgotten within the hour. Second, the act of writing down one idea often sparks more ideas.

WHAT IF?

However bright its spark may be, an idea is not enough to create a story. Something must fan the spark and make it grow. One of the best ways to get that spark going is to ask a question about the idea, and the question is

WHAT IF . . . ?

What if the Three Little Pigs had been the bad guys, always threatening and making life miserable for the poor old Wolf?

What if one morning, just when you were about to take your dog Rufus on a run, he whistled at you and called, "Come on, good kid! Let's go!"?

What if that girl you read about in the magazine really did find an explorer from outer space in her backyard?

PLOT = FRAMEWORK

When you have decided on an idea you like, you have the foundation on which to build your story. Then it is time to think about your framework. The framework of your story is your story plan, or plot. The word *plot* is not something to strike terror to the hearts of new writers. It is merely a plan for putting a story together. You will find almost as many different ways of explaining plot as there are writers. Here are some examples:

Plot is
- development and outcome of a difficult situation
- the path a story follows from beginning to end
- a blueprint for a story
- someone wanting something
- someone wanting something that belongs to someone else.

Robert Newton Peck, author of *A Day No Pigs Would Die,* the *Soup* books, and many others, says that plot is two dogs and one bone, or, in playing musical chairs, two fannies and one chair.[1] It's wanting something that belongs to someone else, and winners mean losers—good losers or poor losers or losers who don't accept defeat. Whatever the bone—money, love, hate—just be sure there are more dogs than bones.

EQUATION FOR A STORY PLAN

Still another description of a story plan is like a math equation. Written this way, it is easy to remember and easy to use.

STORY PLAN = a character + complication + what the character does about it

A complication can range from a nuisance to a dilemma to a catastrophe. It might be a mystery, a puzzle, a goal set by the main character, or a challenge given by someone else. But the problem or complication is just one part of the equation. We need each of the three parts that make up the plot or story plan because

- a *character* without a problem, a goal to achieve, or a challenge to meet wouldn't have anything to do.
- a *problem* without a character involved would be of no interest. It would have no meaning.
- no *effort* to solve the problem or to reach the goal would mean no action, no happenings, no suspense. There would be no story.

Solving a problem involves conflict that can be physical combat, clash of wills or ideas, or unseen struggle within an individual's thoughts. A story based on resolving a mental conflict might not have overt action but still have struggle and suspense. Chapter 3 goes into detail about kinds of problems and their solutions.

THE NEXT QUESTION

After you have found an idea you like and have decided on an answer to the question *What if?*, it is time to ask another question, and this second question is

THEN WHAT?

Some people have filing-cabinet minds with information that is neatly organized and quickly found. Most of us have minds more like a desk piled high with stacks of unsorted, unrelated facts and fancies. When we're looking for answers to the question *Then what?*, the quickest way to sort through this unfiled material is to brainstorm.

BRAINSTORMING SESSIONS

It has been said that everything has been thought of before, so the problem is to think of it again. Or, as Roger von Oech, author of *A Whack on the Side of the Head,* puts it, "Discovery consists of looking at the same thing as everyone else and thinking something different."[2] That is what brainstorming is about.

In a group brainstorming session, a key word or idea is tossed in and those taking part speak up with anything that comes to mind. The rule is that no idea or suggestion is considered too silly or too absurd. Good ideas often bounce off wild ones, and if some ideas make everyone laugh, that's good, too, because researchers say that a bit of humor and playfulness helps to increase creativity.

18

Brainstorming by yourself is another method of looking at things in new ways. Make lists of every possible or impossible idea that you can think up or remember that is related to your subject. But you'll find more ideas if you go deeper than just quick recall allows. Marjorie Holmes, in *Writing Articles from the Heart*, says, "That marvelous instrument, the mind, has for all practical, useful purposes, two layers: the conscious and the unconscious. The writer learns to use both in the begetting of ideas."[3]

One way to explore what the brain has recorded is to use free writing. Choose a subject for a starter and for a short time write quickly and uncritically whatever comes into your head. Then look at what you have written to find ideas, patterns, or thoughts for following further.

Another excellent way of tapping into the unconscious layer of the mind is through the technique called *clustering* (or webbing, branching, patterning, mapping—call it what you choose). In her book *Writing the Natural Way* Gabriele Lusser Rico explains clustering, which is her right-brain method of brainstorming for associations, ideas, metaphors, words, and consequently, for answers to the question *Then what?*

Suppose you've been wondering about that girl who claimed to have a visitor from outer space in her backyard. What if *you* had a space visitor? What problems or complications might it cause? Try clustering for some *Then what?* ideas.

What complications could your talking dog Rufus cause you? If Rufus is to be the main character of your story, what problems might he have?

Or would you like to rewrite the story of the Wolf and the Three Pigs? What would be the Wolf's problem? Don't say just "The Three Little Pigs." You need some specific things the Three Pigs do to torment or frighten the Wolf. To see what other writers have done with folktales, read *The True Story of the Three Little Pigs* by Jon Scieszka, *The Three Little Wolves and the Big Bad Pig* by Eugene Trivizas and Helen Oxenburg, and *Goldilocks and The Three Bears* retold by James Marshall.

CHARACTER, COMPLICATION, AND OUTCOME

Sometimes we hear of a way someone has solved a problem that seems so clever, so unusual, that we say, Hey! That would make a good story. But more often, the first idea for a story comes from a puzzling problem or an interesting character. After you decide on your main character and what the complication is going to be, you'll ask *What If?* and *Then what?* again. You don't need to figure out all the details of your story at this point, but do have a general idea of where the story is going and how it will end.

When you have the three components that add up to make your story plan, you will have the framework on which you'll create your story.

As you use your basic plot or story plan, you'll discover that often the characters in stories you read have the same sorts of problems and solve them in many of the same ways. How can you make your story different? The difference in stories with similar plots lies in the telling. Different authors will tell their stories in quite different ways.

Instead of the Wolf's making life miserable for the Three Little Pigs, or the Third Little Pig making life miserable for the Wolf, the story might be about a neighborhood bully who terrorizes everyone living on the street, or it might be about the brutal dictator of an imaginary country. The details a writer chooses are what make old story plots seem new, and similar story plots seem different.

When you are eager to begin writing, you may be tempted to skip over working out a plan for your story. But give some thought and care to making a strong framework for the general idea of the story before you start on the details. In the long run, a story plan will save you time, make your writing easier, and help you create a story that is not in danger of falling to pieces because of carelessly prepared groundwork.

SIX QUESTIONS

As you begin to work out the details of your story, you'll come up with more questions to ask about the characters, the problem, and the solving of the problem. To answer the questions, we'll ask more questions. The first ones are the Five W's and H. Following chapters will talk about these questions and their answers.

Who?	The characters
What?	The complication or problem
When?	The setting and time
Where?	The place
Why?	Why the characters do what they do
How?	How the main character resolves the complication

SOME THINGS TO THINK ABOUT

We have used the analogy, or comparison, of building houses and creating stories. In the same way the builder needs a foundation to start with, you need an idea. But while the builder can't install windows until the walls are up, you can sometimes be working on details even if your plans aren't complete. Parts of a story often come to us in bits and pieces at various times. Don't depend on remembering story details because they can drift away. If you write them out, they will be there, ready to use when you need them.

Think of some of the stories you've heard over and over. Try turning them around or upside down for new stories. Ask *What if?* and *Then what?* What if the story of the town mouse and the country mouse is changed, so that it's about people instead of mice? What if Rip Van Winkle slept two hundred years instead of twenty? Or came back from his afternoon in the hills to find everyone in his village asleep?

TWO

WHO ARE THE PEOPLE IN YOUR STORY? WHY DO THEY BEHAVE THE WAY THEY DO?

Story Plan = A CHARACTER + a complication +
what character does about it

If your story is to come alive, your characters must be alive. Your reader must be able to see and hear them, to observe how they go about their daily lives, and to understand why they act and react as they do.

That doesn't mean you will use people you know as your characters. It means that you will know the characters you create for your story as well as you know the real people around you. In fact, you'll know them better. This is because in addition to your knowing the characters' names, appearance, and background, you will also know exactly what your characters are thinking and why they do the things they do.

The more you know about your characters, the easier it will be to make your readers feel that they know them, too. If readers aren't interested in the main character of a story—what she does, what happens to him—they won't be interested in the story.

GETTING ACQUAINTED—CHARACTER CHARTS

One of the best and easiest ways to get acquainted with a character is to make a character chart. A chart is not for creating characters. You do that as you plan your story. The chart is to help you learn more about the characters. Knowing what they look like and where they live is not enough. You need to get inside their thoughts and feelings, share their hopes and fears. When you have completed a character chart or one of its alternatives, you will not only know who your characters are, you will also know why they are who they are. The more important a character is, the more details you'll want.

Characters' names are one of the first things to enter on the charts, but the names are not necessarily the first things you know about your characters. Finding the exactly right name is often a matter of trying and trying again. Choose a working name for each character while you hunt for the name that truly fits.

MORE QUESTIONS

If you want to know more about your characters, you can answer personal questions:

- What are this character's favorite books, music, sports, food?
- What are this character's daydreams? Strongest memories?
- Who are this character's personal heroes?
- What do friends say about the character?
- What do enemies say about the character?

CHARACTER CHART

Is your character a man, woman, boy, girl, animal, or a fantasy character?

Name: (Give your characters names as soon as you begin your story, but be free to change those names if you think of better ones.)

PHYSICAL DESCRIPTION

Age: (Give actual age of children and teenagers, a general idea of age for adults—early twenties, middle age, elderly.)
Height & Weight:
Eyes:
Hair:
Special Physical Abilities or Disabilities: (Only if important to story.)

ENVIRONMENT AND ACTIVITIES

Time Setting: (Such as Paleolithic Period, 1492, 3492, etc.)
Place: (Mars, southern France, Chicago, a Montana ranch, etc.)
Home: (Castle, apartment, wigwam, etc.)
Who Shares This Home?: (Family, elderly uncle, fifteen cats, etc.)
Immediate Family Relationships: (Parents? Brothers or sisters? Grandparents? No immediate family?)
Place in Family: (Head of household, middle child, only child, foster child, etc.)

Friends:
Pets:
Occupation: (If appropriate.)
School: (If appropriate. Does character go to school? Inner-city school, private school, one-room country school? What grade?)
After-school Job: (If appropriate.)
Hobbies and Special Interests:

PERSONAL THOUGHTS, FEELINGS, ATTITUDES

Disposition: (Happy, nervous, curious, etc.)
How Does Character Feel About Himself or Herself:
How Does Character Feel About Friends:
How Does Character Feel About Family:
How Does Character Feel About Job or School: (Include feelings about employer, fellow employees, teachers, best-liked and least-liked subjects.)
Ambitions:

PERSONALITY TRAITS

What is Character's Dominant Personality Trait:
What is Character's Secondary Personality Trait:

CHARACTER GROWTH

Does Character Change Ideas, Beliefs, or Attitudes as a Result of Experiences in the Course of the Story:
In What Ways: (You may not be able to answer this until you've worked on your story for a while.)

Another way to find out more about people is to play the game of comparisons. What would your character be if he or she were a

vegetable	gemstone	musical instrument
flower	song	piece of furniture
animal	color	article of clothing

Add your own ideas to the list and use them to develop impressions of your characters:

Kate is a pine tree.   Bert is a Chevy pickup.
Sean is a dictionary.   Mrs. Biddle is a chick-
                           adee.

OTHER WAYS TO GET ACQUAINTED

Rather than a chart, you may prefer to write biographical sketches about the characters. These will vary from several sentences to several pages, depending on the importance of the character. Some writers make up journals for their characters. Others cover their bulletin boards with magazine pictures that look like their characters and their settings.
Try making lists of information:

Cinderella is the kind of person who
    lets people take advantage of her
    is kind to mice
    likes to stay out late

Mrs. O'Malley is the kind of person who
    says hello to strange dogs
    still avoids stepping on cracks
    goes to a different church every Sunday

After you have learned a little bit about your character, try setting up situations and write a paragraph in which the character argues with someone, shows anger or concern, or tries to explain something. These might not go into your story but could bring out facets of personality that hadn't occurred to you before.

PERSONALITY TRAITS

One of the chart questions asks about a character's dominant personality trait. That strongest trait is more important than the character's appearance or background or position in life, and it is necessary to know what it is before you start to write your story. The dominant personality trait will influence the way your character thinks, acts, reacts, and finally solves the problems in the story.

Here is a starter list of possible traits for you to add to:

ambitious	honest
boastful	kind
brave	lazy
careless	loving
cheerful	loyal
conceited	persevering
cruel	proud
curious	secretive
dishonest	selfish
generous	shy
gloomy	suspicious
greedy	wasteful

The amount of detail for each character depends not only on importance and age of the character, but also on the age of the reader and the length of the story. Even a three-hundred-word story about three-year-old Susie's first trip to the zoo needs background information. Does Susie have a stuffed-animal zoo at home and does she want to see a real, live elephant? Or is she afraid of animals? Is the adult taking her bored, annoyed, or as excited as Susie?

LIFE CLASS

Sometimes artists make detailed drawings of their models. Other times, they use the model to see anatomical structure, light and shadow, posture, or mood. Will you ever use real people as models? Yes and no. Even if you want a duplicate of Cousin Jeff, you'll find that by the time he filters through your thoughts and adapts to the circumstances of your story, his own mother won't recognize him. But use care. If it is Cousin Jeff's personality you want, then give the character someone else's looks and a different name.

There is another reason not to use a photocopy of Cousin Jeff. You want your characters to seem real and alive, but real people are far too complex and too inconsistent to fit into the limitations of a story. Good fictional characters are simplified versions of real people. Simplified, yes, but at the same time they are also a little larger than life.

Art is not reality but the illusion of reality.

THE PRIMARY PERSONALITY TRAIT

The fictional character will have one dominant characteristic, such as generosity, curiosity, courage, or selfishness, laziness, dishonesty. This does not mean the character is all good or all bad, but that the motivation, attitude, and behavior will develop from one primary personality trait.

Your heroes will make mistakes, lose their tempers, or say tactless things. Your villains may forget themselves and be kind to small animals or drop coins in the Salvation Army kettle. These slips will be typical of human weakness. It is through these lapses, and the embarrassment, remorse, or unhappiness they cause the character who makes them, that real people can understand and sympathize with fictional people.

Such slips, however, must not be inconsistent with the character's primary personality trait. A truly honest person will not slip up and do a little embezzling now and then; Santa Claus will not go out and kick the reindeer.

People in real life act out of character with unsettling frequency, but your story will lose strength and direction if your characters do not act consistently with their personalities.

SECONDARY TRAITS

Choose contrasts but consistent contrasts for primary and secondary traits. Perhaps Janie is bright and creative, but a small streak of laziness keeps her from following through and making something of her ideas.

Mr. Willoby has a sharp, analytical mind that solves problems and finds answers quickly, yet his shyness often keeps him from speaking up. Both Janie and Mr. Willoby have two battles to fight: the problem they face in the plot of the story and the conflict they face within themselves.

TWO SIDES TO THE COIN

Personality traits can be double-sided. People have the faults of their virtues. "Generous to a fault" is more than just a cliché. Frankness can become tactlessness; firmness can be stubbornness; the born leader may turn into a dictator; the retiring person, into a hermit.

The trait that leads your hero to final victory can also, with a secondary personality trait, cause setbacks along the way. The adventurous person acts without thinking, the cautious person holds back until opportunity is almost lost.

The dominant personality trait is more important than a character's appearance, background, or position, because this core quality will be apparent to greater or lesser degree in everything the character does and says.

WHAT DO YOUR CHARACTERS DO?

Think of your story as a play. All the characters who walk onstage have jobs, large or small, to do, or they must not be there. Your characters must earn a place in your story.

As you build your cast, think about the character's contribution to the plot.

Is it a leading role?
Main character, hero, protagonist—one who takes the lead in a cause
Villain, or at least antagonist—one who opposes the protagonist

Is it a minor role?
A minor character who helps to stir up conflict or diversion

A minor character who, like a Greek Chorus, helps to explain and interpret what is happening

MINOR CHARACTERS

Keep a careful eye on your minor characters. Too many can be confusing, so don't crowd the stage. If Tom's only part in the story is to deliver the morning paper, then don't give him a name. Call him the paper boy, or, as Tom, let him also be the one to see the mysterious stranger or to find the missing letter instead of giving those jobs to Dick or Harry.

Don't let minor characters become stereotypes. Not all police officers are Irish. Not all police are men. Give them small habits or personality quirks that the reader will recognize and remember. "Bernadine arrived in her usual cloud of gardenia perfume." A dozen pages later, the reader may have forgotten Bernadine's name but will remember that whiff of gardenia.

All of your characters, major or minor, by their actions and reactions to each other, help to develop each other's personalities.

The waitress, setting down a glass, splashed water on the manuscript and Joe swore.

The waitress, setting down a glass, splashed water on the manuscript. Joe blotted it with a napkin and reassured her, "No problem. My editor says it's too dry anyway."

Unless that waitress turns out to be Joe's long-lost mother, she'll probably never be seen again, so she will have no name and no characteristics, but she has played a role in helping us to know more about Joe.

Do your characters provide contrast for each other? The comedian has a straight man, Laurel has Hardy, Punch has Judy. Cinderella is sweet and gentle, her stepsisters are selfish and conniving. The same is true for King Lear's daughters, Cordelia versus Goneril and Regan. Contrast in characters adds both color and conflict to your story.

WHAT DO YOUR CHARACTERS WANT?

You have a clear idea of each character's job in the development of your plot. But have you worked out the goal or goals each character will try to achieve?

Is it a positive or a negative goal? Is it sufficiently difficult to achieve?

Are there other goals that clash with it, causing conflict, tension, suspense?

The Big Bad Wolf's goal is to eat up the Three Little Pigs. The Third Little Pig's goal is to escape from the Wolf.

Do your characters also have secondary goals?

The Third Little Pig's secondary goals were to get turnips from Mr. Smith's Home-field, apples from the tree at Merry-garden, and a churn from the fair. These goals put the Pig in more danger and cause more conflict.

But conflict leads to growth. Your characters learn as they try and try again. By the end of the story a character should have changed, matured, grown in some way because of what has happened. This would not be a sudden conversion, an unbelievable reversal of the character's values, but it should be a few steps in a new direction. And if your story is successful, it may start some thinking in a new direction for your reader as well.

WHAT'S IN A NAME?

Give your characters names as soon as you start your story, but be free to change them. Find names that will help your reader identify the characters. Be careful that they don't all begin with the same letter or sound or look too much alike, unless that is part of your story plan. Jean and Gene don't look alike but sound the same. Jean and Joan don't sound alike but look similar enough to confuse the reader.

Think about the time and place of the story you are writing and about the type of story when you select names. Sid Fleischman, in *Jingo Django*, named some of his characters General Scurlock, Mr. Hemlock, and Billy Bottles. Ruth Riddell's *Haunted Journey*, a story about rural Tennessee in the early part of the 1930s, has characters named Obie and Delsi Wilks, Bas Allardice, and Bub Torrey. In her book about present-day kids and racing cars, *Red-Hot Wheels*, her characters are named Greg, Danny, BJ, and Kelly.

For help with names, look in a what-to-name-the-baby book, the biographical section of a dictionary or a biographical dictionary, or the telephone book.

NAMES OF REAL PEOPLE

Use caution with names of real people. If you use the telephone book for help, find a first name in one place, a last name in another. Be just as cautious using names of people you know. No matter how wonderful your hero might be, the person whose name you use could be embarrassed or upset.

TAGS TO HELP YOUR READER

Another way to help readers get acquainted with your characters is to use character tags. These are brief descriptions of the way characters look or act or talk. You've already met Bernadine and her gardenia perfume, but there are other senses to use, too.

Chris bounded in the door, yelling as always.

Aunt Lucy was wearing her favorite color, peacock blue. This time it was a velour running suit trimmed with shocking pink.

Speech trademarks are another way to identify characters:

Uncle Harry always began, "Well, uh, as I see it . . ."

Billy talked so fast that his words doubled up on each other.

Action habits can make characters seem real:

Mr. Green checked his watch before he answered. He always did that.

Grandma wandered about the kitchen, opening cupboards and pulling out drawers as she questioned me.

YOUR READER MEETS YOUR CHARACTERS

By now you know your characters quite well, so it is time to think about how you will show them to your reader. Of course you, as author, can describe them, but story characters will seem more real if your readers hear them and watch them in action.

Showing a character doing something in keeping with a personality trait will give the reader a better picture and more understanding of that character than any description of height, weight, color of eyes or hair.

> *Evelyn Couch had locked herself in her sewing room and was eating a second pint of Baskin-Robbins chocolate chip ice cream. . .*
>
> *She had lied to the boy at Baskin-Robbins. She told him that the ice cream was for a party for her grandchildren. She didn't even have any grandchildren.[1]*
> —Fannie Flagg, *Fried Green Tomatoes at the Whistle Stop Cafe*

Other effective ways to help your reader know a character include comments and reactions from others and the character's own statements or thoughts.

> *I didn't come to Utah to be the same boy I'd been before. I had my own dreams of transformation, Western dreams, dreams of freedom and dominion and taciturn self-sufficiency. The first thing I wanted to do was change my name . . . I wanted to call myself Jack, after Jack London.[2]*
> —Tobias Wolff, *This Boy's Life*

You won't want to reveal everything about a character as soon as the story opens, so let your readers get to know the characters gradually, just as your characters get to know each other gradually.

WHICH CHARACTER TELLS THE STORY?

As you think about the characters in your story, decide whose story it is. If it is a story about Ann's wanting to run in the May Relays, then Ann will be the main character. If it is a story in which Ann, Ben, and Cassie are putting out a class newspaper, decide which one of the three will be the main character.

When you have chosen the main character, tell the story from that person's point of view. That means you will tell the story the way that person sees it, thinks about it, feels about it.

Books, especially books for adults, often tell stories from the viewpoint of various people, but short stories and children's books are usually told from the viewpoint of just one character.

If you decide that Ben is your main character, you might tell the story this way:

We didn't ask for it, but Ann, Cassie, and I got stuck with the job of putting out the class newspaper.

I didn't know what Ann and Cassie thought, but I knew I wanted to be out shooting baskets with the guys.

This "I" way of telling is called *first person*. You tell the story as if you were the main character.

You might prefer telling Ben's story in *third person*. Ben is still the main character, but instead of being *I*, becomes *he*.

Ann, Cassie, and Ben were given the job of putting out the class newspaper. Ben didn't know what the other two were thinking, but he knew he didn't want to be stuck . . .

Ben, as the viewpoint character, can know only what his senses tell him or what someone else tells him. He can't know what another character is thinking, although he might guess. He can't see that he himself looks worried or happy or embarrassed unless he has a mirror handy, but he might realize that he looks worried by the reaction of others. He cannot know what is happening on the other side of town until someone brings him the news.

Once in a great while you may find a story told in second person. Second person is you.

So! You got stuck with the job of putting out the paper. Just your luck. But you went in after school, and there were Ann and Cassie waiting . . .

Another way of telling a story is with omniscient viewpoint. (Omniscient: knowing everything.) With an omniscient point of view, the storyteller is at a distance, seeing everything that happens and knowing what each character is thinking and doing.

Ann, Ben, and Cassie were given the job of putting out the class newspaper. Ann was not happy. She'd planned to spend every free hour after school training for May Relays. Ben didn't want to work on the paper, either. He'd rather be out shooting baskets with the guys. And Cassie, well, Cassie was disappointed. She wanted to work on the paper, but she'd expected to be named editor in chief. That

*way she'd have been able to make all the
decisions herself.*

You might want to experiment with the omniscient
viewpoint after you've written several stories from
first-person or third-person point of view. Frequently,
books are written in multiple viewpoint with the story
told by various characters as they see it happening.
But unless each change of viewpoint is clearly estab-
lished by using a drop-down of several spaces or by
starting a new chapter, the reader will be confused.
You will help your reader identify with the main character and become a part of the action if you tell your
story from just one character's point of view.

After you have written the first draft, you might
decide that a different viewpoint would be better.
While the viewpoint character is usually the main
character, occasionally stories are told from a
bystander's point of view. Experiment until you find
the right viewpoint character and the right kind of
viewpoint for that character.

SOME THINGS TO THINK ABOUT

You won't include everything that you've found out
about the characters in your story, but the more you
know about them, the more skillfully you will be able
to show how they talk and act and think. When your
characters are real and alive to your readers, then
your stories, too, will be real and alive.

*One of the strangest quirks of the human
mind is its capacity for being moved to tears,
laughter, anger, anxiety, joy by a "person"
who exists nowhere except in imagination!
The explanation is "identity." . . . The reader*

identifies with the imaginary individual invent-ed by the author—in effect becomes that per-son, seeing what he sees, hearing what he hears, experiencing what he experiences, hoping what he hopes.[3]

—Jane Fitz-Randolph,
How to Write for Children
& Young Adults

THREE

WHAT'S THE PROBLEM AND HOW DOES IT GET SOLVED?

Story Plan = a character + A COMPLICATION + what character does about it

When you decided on an idea and asked *What if?*, you prepared the foundation for your story. When you created characters to go with that idea you started building the framework. Now, as you discover what your main character's situation or complication or problem is, you will add to the framework.

WANTS AND NEEDS

In getting acquainted with your characters, a question you asked about each one was *What does this character want?* When you find the specific answer to that question and what it is that keeps the character from getting it, then you have the next part of your story framework. You have your character's problem.

In thinking about that problem, remember the word *specific*. Abstract terms such as *wisdom, success,* or *happiness* won't do. People have lots of wants, and these wants come from the areas of our basic needs for security.

Physical security — food, clothing, shelter, health, safety

Social relationships — approval and esteem, membership in a group

Personal and emotional — friendship, affection, relationships love

Mental security — knowledge and understanding

Philosophical or — belief, faith in spiritual security something beyond self

The Three Little Pigs want physical security. So does the Wolf. The girl with the spaceship in her yard might be in some physical danger. Certainly, she needs to have her friends believe her; otherwise both her social and mental security are also at risk.

Wants and needs can be as everyday and commonplace as Susie's trying to find someone to play with on a Saturday afternoon, or they can be as kingdom-shaking as Richard the Third's fighting to save his throne.

Whether readers will care about Mr. Wolf, Susie, or Richard the Third will depend on the emotions involved. If, through their own experiences, they can relate to the problems, then those readers will be concerned about what the character does and what happens to him or her. They will be concerned, that is, if the problem itself is important enough. Someone has said there's nothing very dramatic about a fall from a footstool. The more your character has to win or lose, the higher your reader's interest and emotional involvement will be.

CONFLICT

Conflict does not necessarily mean violence. It can be physical, or it can be mental or emotional. Conflict leads to action and suspense, and both are necessary to make a story.

When you know what your character wants, the next step is to ask *Why can't the character have it?* What the character wants and what keeps him or her from getting it create conflict, and human beings, real or fictional, face three kinds of conflict:

- The individual against nature, the supernatural, or things beyond human control.
- The individual against another individual or society.
- The individual against himself or herself.

Let's take an example: A man is scaling a sheer rock face. Such a climb is, in itself, a challenge with its own difficulties. It could make a story. But let's add more problems.

Joe is driving up a mountain road that runs beside a swiftly moving creek. Every few miles he sees warning signs that say IN CASE OF FLOOD CLIMB TO HIGH GROUND. Climbing up the face of a rocky cliff is far from Joe's mind. But as he enters a narrow canyon he sees that the creek is rising, running over its banks and onto the road. He remembers the posted signs. This is a gullywasher, no doubt caused by a cloudburst farther up the mountain. Joe has no choice but to climb. He leaves his car and starts to scramble up the steep canyon wall. He's not a rock climber—that's one difficulty. The water is rising rapidly. That's a second difficulty. And night is falling as rapidly as the water is rising. That's a third difficulty. Joe is truly in conflict with nature, and he has problems.

Or, for whatever reason, it is important to Joe that one Saturday afternoon he climb a certain rock face. He's a good climber, and he knows if he is careful and concentrates on what he is doing, he can make it. But up above him, his worst enemy appears and starts throwing rocks down. Joe is definitely in conflict with another person, although at this point we don't know why.

Or, as a third example, let's say that Joe wants to climb. He's taken climbing lessons. He has all the proper gear. He's climbing with an experienced mentor. He wants to prove to himself that he can do it. But Joe is deathly afraid of heights. Joe is in conflict with himself.

Conflicts do not have to be hostile, involving attacks or assaults. A difficulty might arise from a competition or from a misunderstanding that is not life-threatening. Characters do not always fall neatly into the roles of hero or villain. But when another character is keeping your main character from realizing a goal, you need to know when and what that second character wants. When you have your character's goal based on a want or a need, and when you have a strong reason why he or she can't reach that goal, then you have your character's problem and a good second piece of framework for your story. Now you are ready to put the third part of the framework into place.

SOLUTIONS

Story Plan = a character + a complication + WHAT
CHARACTER DOES ABOUT IT

When you have a problem for your character, the next question is *What does the character do about the problem?* If the character decides to do nothing, making that decision is doing *something*, but it probably won't lead to a very strong story. If your character's goal is important enough, he or she will be motivated to go after it in spite of obstacles.

Now there is another question to ask: *How does the character solve the problem?* Again it is necessary to be specific.

How can the Third Little Pig get rid of the Wolf?
How can Joe stop the person from throwing rocks at him and safely finish his climb?

The answer to your problem-question is your *solution*, and this is what makes your story. The characters may be great, the problem may be even greater, but the story is going nowhere until the action starts, and that is what happens when, win or lose, the protagonist does something specific about the problem. If there is no attempt, there is no action, and so there is no story.

Action won't all be dragon-slaying. It differs, depending on the story's situation and characters. It might take place in the main character's thoughts and be the process of working out a problem or misunderstanding. But even with such quiet action, the character still must do *something* as a result of the thinking or planning. Having resolved the problem mentally, the character can roll over and go to sleep. Or, having recognized a misunderstanding, the character goes out determined to make things right once more.

Good solutions, solutions satisfying to the reader, must develop out of the situation and out of the character traits of protagonist and antagonist.

Keep in mind, too, that the main character will

have secondary personality traits and that any trait can have a reverse side. Think about your character's weakest personality trait. What is the worst thing that could happen because of that weak trait?

Remember Ann, Ben, and Cassie, who were supposed to put out the class newspaper? Cassie, who wanted the job of editor in chief, has lots of clever ideas but is inclined to ignore the suggestions of others. Ben, too, is creative, but he's careless about promptness and deadlines. Ann has ambitious plans for the paper but can't be bothered with working out details for accomplishing them. What conflicts could these personality clashes cause?

Think about your characters' personalities as you plan your solution. Think, too, about these don'ts and do's:

- Don't depend on coincidence to solve the problem. Joe won't just happen to find a laser slingshot on a ledge of the cliff and use it to blast his enemy.
- Don't bring in some last-minute person or power to save the day. The ancient Greek theater used this method, which is called *deus ex machina*, a god from a machine. A character representing one of the gods was lowered onto the stage by a crane or other device in order to save the characters. The woodcutter who appears in the nick of time to save Grandma and Little Red Riding Hood is a good example of *deus ex machina*. This is too convenient, and not an acceptable method of problem solving.
- Don't untangle everything by having your main character announce, "And then I woke up. It was all a dream." This cheats your reader out of the most important part of the story, that of seeing how the main character manages to win out over difficulties.

Dreams can be used effectively in stories. Lewis

Carroll, in *Alice's Adventures in Wonderland* and also in *Through the Looking Glass*, tells complete stories within the framework of Alice's dreams. A student writer's main character used a dream about outwitting a villain as the pattern for outwitting an adversary in real life. And in Dickens's *A Christmas Carol*, Scrooge's dreams, if they were dreams, convince him to change his real-life behavior. Heroes must find ways out of their troubles. Saying, "And then I woke up," when the moment is blackest is not the way to solve a problem.

- Do be sure that your main character is the one who works out the solution.
- Do create suspense by keeping your character from reaching the goal too quickly or too easily.
- Do remember that for every action there is a reaction. When your protagonist does something to solve the problem, your antagonist will do something to block it. The first attempt to solve the problem should lead to complications and more problems. More attempts will take the protagonist even farther from the goal. Will he succeed—or won't he?

SUSPENSE

Every story has two possible endings: the ending your reader hopes will happen and the ending your reader fears will happen. To these two elements, hope and fear, we add one more: a time limit. Will the character succeed—in time?

Charlotte Armstrong, a prolific writer of mysteries, called *hope, fear,* and *time* the three balls we must keep juggling in order to create suspense. And we're not talking of suspense just in mystery or adventure stories. Every story must have some sort of tension or suspense to keep the reader reading. Whether it is the horror of a Stephen King novel or the determination of *The Little Engine That Could*, a story moves forward on degrees of hope and fear and time. *Moves forward* are key words as well as *hope, fear,* and *time*. The problem-solving must never stand still.

Remember Joe's enemy up at the top of the cliff? When your character gets too close to the goal, throw some rocks. Push the character back. A seeming failure builds tension. The more the reader cares about your character, the more that reader will be concerned about the jeopardy (physical, mental, or psychological) you put the character in. Care and concern build tension and suspense. And suspense keeps your reader reading.

THE DARKEST MOMENT

The old saying about it being darkest just before the dawn holds true for your character and his or her problem. Each attempt to find a solution leads to more difficulties. A point will come when unraveling the mystery or clearing up the misunderstanding or achieving the goal seems hopeless. But your character makes one last, valiant effort. It might be a physical effort, or the dawning awareness of a fact or happening encountered earlier. Or the character may see the situation from a new perspective and, realizing something that provides an answer, make the move that saves the day. The problem is solved, the goal is attained.

SOME THINGS TO THINK ABOUT

What does your character want?
What keeps your character from getting it?
Does your character have the motivation to go after it anyway?

If your answer to this last question is no, go directly to jail, do not pass go, do not collect two hundred dollars, because if there is no motivation to act, there is no story.

If your answer is yes, go ahead, work out the details, because you now have the solid foundation and the strong framework for a story.

FOUR

WHEN DOES ALL THIS HAPPEN AND WHERE?

WHEN and WHERE are not included in the plot equation, but they are vital to the development of a story. The combination of when a story takes place and where it takes place is usually referred to as *setting* or *background*. But setting is more than scenery, and the atmosphere of a setting is affected by more than just the where and the when. To these two, we add the social, cultural, moral, and economic influences of that particular time and place. An inclusive term for all of this is *environment*.

THE ENVIRONMENT OF A STORY

The *Oxford American Dictionary* gives a definition of environment as *surroundings, especially those affecting people's lives*. Story characters, to be convincing, must seem like real, living, and breathing people, not just actors posing in front of painted backdrops. To live and breathe, these characters must exist in a real environment, that is, one that seems real to the reader.

You want your reader to know that when characters go out a door, they are going out into real streets and about real business, that they are not just standing in the wings waiting for their next cues. When a character opens a window, you want your reader to hear the street noises, feel the breeze, or smell the scents of the garden just outside.

If you are writing a present-day story, your readers will automatically fill in much of the information from their own experiences. With historical stories or stories with foreign settings, you'll need to provide more information about the place and the customs. In science fiction and fantasy, you may have to create a whole new world. But however much or little information you provide, be sure it is consistent and accurate.

WHAT ROLE DOES YOUR SETTING PLAY?

Settings are always important, but some settings play leading roles in their stories, and others, while adding reality and color, are not necessary to the actual plot.

Certain stories remain the same no matter where or when they take place. Almost every country in the world has some version of the Cinderella story in its folklore. The idea of O. Henry's "The Gift of the Magi" has been used over and over with different casts of characters and different backgrounds. In this type of story, the plot can be picked up and put down in a new locale without changing the basic idea. New characters and new settings make an old plot into a new story.

Sometimes the setting is so important that the story could happen only in that one place and time. Tom Sawyer and Huckleberry Finn would have been quite different boys had they grown up in a New

England fishing village or in a western frontier town instead of on the banks of the Mississippi River. Nor would the characters of *The Wind in the Willows* or of the L. M. Boston *Green Knowe* books be the same if their homes had been the Mississippi instead of their own rivers. Their regional settings are essential parts of their stories.

Then there are stories that use setting, either natural or created, as the antagonist in the plot. These are the character-versus-environment stories, and they include

- character challenging environment
- character attempting to conquer his or her environment
- character attempting to escape from an environment
- character attempting to stay alive in a dangerous or strange environment

WHAT IS GOING ON IN YOUR STORY'S WORLD?

Whether setting is a leading actor in your story or is background for other kinds of action, you need to know what is happening in the world where your story takes place.

Has gold been discovered in California? Are explorers sailing to the edge of the world without falling off? Are explorers mapping outer space? What would the newspaper headlines be? What's on MTV? Along with the century and the year, think of the time of year, the season. And don't forget to check the weather report. Climate and weather can influence people's lives. You won't use all of this information in your story, but knowing the details will help you create the environment in which the story takes place.

HOW TO INCLUDE YOUR READER

You have lots of information about your setting, but one more thing is necessary. You need to put your readers into your story, right along with your characters. You don't want readers looking on from a distance or just listening as you describe a time and a place. You want to take readers there, too. How do you do it? The answer is

SHOW, DON'T TELL

You bring information alive for the reader by making the details *sensory*—not only how the scenery looks, but how things sound and smell and taste, how things feel to the touch, and, yes, how they feel to the heart and the memory.

Telling is using indefinite, abstract words: a nice spring day, an old house, a cold morning.

If we write, It was cold and the sidewalk was covered with snow, that sentence merely tells.

Showing is using concrete, sensory details that make pictures and stir readers' memories, reminding them of personal experiences.

Joan Aiken, in the opening of *The Wolves of Willoughby Chase*, writes,

> *It was dusk—winter dusk. Snow lay white and shining over the pleated hills, and icicles hung from the forest trees.*[1]

Poet Aileen Fisher added sound:

> *The crisp white snow*
> *Had a soda-cracker crunch.*[2]

Now for a contradiction. To bring your readers

quickly into a story you'll use details, sensory details, but you can bring them in even more easily and quickly if you limit those details.

Let's suppose we need to describe a shabby, run-down house. First we avoid opinion words:

The house looked like —
The house seemed to be —

Second, we'll avoid the abstract words:

old, dilapidated, shabby, run-down

These merely tell. We want to show the readers so they see this house. So we give the readers a few specific details:

peeling paint
kicked-out screen door
gate hanging on one hinge

Then the readers, from their own experiences, will fill in more details. One person might, in imagination, add broken porch railings and a piece of cardboard covering the broken windowpane. Another reader might see the worn-out grass and trash in the yard.

When we let a reader share in describing the house or furnishing a room or reproducing a city street, then that house or room or street comes alive because the reader has helped to create it, and now is taking part in your story.

How much detail is enough?

Put yourself in your character's place. You and he or she are not cameras. When you go into a room do you actually notice every detail? For the details in a description, pinpoint, don't catalog; be specific, don't generalize. Say that it is a sparrow, not just that it's a bird. A vase of flowers on the teacher's desk? A fistful of dandelions drooping over the sides of a jelly glass.

And how about that sparrow that isn't just a bird? What does it sound like?

Annie Dillard wrote,

> *Chipped notes of birdsong descend from the trees, tuneful and broken; the notes pile about me like leaves.*[3]

And Jane Langton said it this way:

> *In the elm tree a hoarse-throated bird had sprung a leak in his kettle and was dripping rusty splashes of song on the lawn.*[4]

By using sensory words, sound, smell, taste, touch, and sight, you will be writing about the emotional response of your character to his or her environment. You'll also be working for an emotional response from your reader. By pointing out commonplace details, you will be inviting feelings and memories from your reader's own experiences. You can't evoke emotion by calling it by its name. You need the sensory details that touch a feeling, a memory, of the reader's. And to make these responses as real as possible, use the ones you know best—your own memories and feelings and responses.

PUT YOUR SETTINGS TO WORK

What are you going to do with these descriptions you write? Well, you're not going to just toss huge chunks of them on every other page. Today readers won't sit still for thousands of words of description the way readers did one or two hundred years ago. And you won't deliver descriptions several pages at a time because you'll be putting small pieces of them to work, doing more than just the job of describing setting.

First, your descriptions of setting will be doing their main job of establishing time and place and general environment for your story. But bits of that same information can help tell your story in several other ways.

DESCRIPTION THAT PROVIDES INFORMATION

A second use for setting description is to make sure the reader will see and know certain details important to the story. These might be stage properties such as a tree growing at the edge of a ravine or Mr. Murphy's pocket watch. If a reflection seen in the hall mirror is necessary to the plot, be sure that the mirror is mentioned the first time your characters go into the hall. Or it might be necessary for the reader to know a certain fact. If the distance from one town to another is important, include that in your description.

DESCRIPTION TO HEIGHTEN EMOTION

A third way to put descriptive passages to work is by using them to interrupt dialogue or action to heighten the emotion of a scene.

Mr. Willburn asked, "And what did Nate Vogel have to say?"

Surely there was something else they could talk about, Betts thought. But Mr. Willburn was like a schoolteacher. He asked a question and you had to answer.

They were coming to the bridge now. The surface of the narrow suspension bridge was

even rougher and more worn than the high-
way. Mr. Willburn seemed to be concentrating
very carefully on his driving.

Betts tried not to see the great outcrop-
pings of jagged rock, shining wet in the rain.
She tried not to look down into the shadows
of the dark canyon to the pewter gray water
hundreds of feet below.

To ease the sick feeling in her stomach she
answered, "Oh, just that he has copies of
papers—important papers."

The car swerved.[5]

—Kathleen C. Phillips,
Sounds in the Dark of the Night

DESCRIPTION TO ESTABLISH MOOD

Establishing the mood of a scene is a fourth way to
use setting description. Would Edgar Allan Poe's stories be the same without their dreary landscapes or
dark, rat-infested prison cells or forgotten cellars?
Imagine *Wuthering Heights* without the moors or the
gloomy old houses. Moods can be light as well as
dark, and descriptions can set the scene for happy
anticipation as well as for dread, for fun and humor
as well as mystery or horror.

It snowed hard all Friday night, letting up at
dawn. Katie went out into the Saturday-morn-
ing sunshine to explore a sparkling world
magically turned to white and gold.[6]

Later in the same story and creating quite a different mood is the description of another snowy
Saturday.

As far as Katie could see, from her bed-
room window, from the front door and the

back, everything—clothesline, electric power poles, fences, sheds, houses, and every branch of every tree—was wrapped with soft, woolly snow. No whisper of wind disturbed even a single snowflake in the silent gray-and-white world. Color and sound were equally muffled by the white blanket. By one o'clock, wheel tracks and footprints scarred the snow, and clumps of it slid from branches with soft plops, but the strange quietness lasted.[7]

—Kathleen C. Phillips,
*Katie McCrary and the
Wiggins Crusade*

If you are planning a bleak or gory or catastrophic happening, you might start off with a bleak day for your setting. Or the day could begin bright and fair and gradually turn gray and stormy as the event approaches. Or the day could stay sunny in contrast to the dark things happening. But you want to be subtle in using devices such as these, because they can easily get out of hand and become melodramatic.

John Lutz, in an article titled "Setting for Suspense," pokes fun at too much mood setting:

Rain burst in violent clichés against the windowpanes, wind whistled hackneyed through the ancient eaves. . . .[8]

DESCRIPTION TO SHOW CHARACTERIZATION

Last, let's see how descriptions of setting can show something about the characters themselves. Rooms and houses, gardens and yards are the most personal of settings, and they can tell us the most about the people who live and work there.

Members of a high school writing workshop wrote descriptions of their own rooms as if being seen by someone else. Two girls had almost identical descriptions. One girl saw her room as looking lived in and cozy. The other girl saw the room she had described as a room belonging to a slob. This exercise not only told something about the girls (and perhaps about their families), but it led to another way in which setting can be used to show a character's personality.

What could we learn about several characters from the different ways in which they view the same setting?

Imagine three people watching children at play in a schoolyard. One is a teenage school dropout; one is a mother whose only child will start school in another year; one is a retired but still dedicated teacher. What would each of these people be seeing, hearing, thinking, feeling, or remembering?

How would the city on a rainy November day seem to a man who has just lost his job? To a man who has just found a job?

We can show a person's character by the home setting. We can contrast characters by their different reactions to a same setting. And a third way we can use setting to develop a character is to show how that character acts and reacts to an environment. This can be as dramatic as Robinson Crusoe in his character-versus-environment struggle to stay alive, but it can also be used in less dramatic situations.

How does a child feel about her big yard with its trees and bushes, places to hide and explore, on a sunny morning?

How does she feel about that same yard when she must go out and rescue a forgotten toy as darkness falls?

Description is best when it has a definite purpose and is not being used for mere decoration. So you'll put your descriptions to work. You'll make them sensory—not just how things look, but how they sound and smell and taste, how they feel to the touch. You'll think about the memories and feelings they evoke.

Most important of all, you will put your characters into your setting and not just pose them in front of a two-dimensional piece of scenery. When your setting is real, your reader will follow your characters into it, to live your story with them.

SOME THINGS TO THINK ABOUT

Author Lesley Conger, in an essay about artists and their memorable illustrations for children's books, concludes with this:

> *A funny thing happened to me when I first started thinking about writing this piece. I went to the bookshelves in my daughters' rooms and looked through all their books to refresh my memory of the illustrations. I looked at poor Alice. . . . I looked at Stuart Little. . . . And finally, I took down my old copy of* The Secret Garden, *the one my mother gave me when I was ten years old. I could see the pictures already, in my head: Ben Weatherstaff spading the earth, with the robin perched boldly on a clod at his feet; Mary finding the door when the ivy blows aside in the wind; the inside of Dickon's cottage, all cozy and delightful; Colin standing up and showing Ben his legs, straight as anyone's.*
>
> *The pages flipped by under my thumb, first one direction then the other, and I blinked. There aren't any pictures in my copy of* The Secret Garden, *none at all.*[9]

The title of Ms. Conger's essay is "The Magic of Pictures, The Magic of Words." Never underestimate the magic of the words you have to choose from, the words you have to make pictures with.

FIVE

ARE YOU READY TO WRITE?

Before starting to work, a builder knows what kind of house the plans call for. When laying the foundation and putting up the framework, the builder knows whether the project is a one-story cottage, a three-story Victorian, or an A-frame. You, as a writer, can have the best of idea-foundation and story-plan-framework but still not know what kind of story this work will turn into.

Your story might be a mystery or adventure in which the protagonist, facing a strong antagonist, tries and tries again, comes to the darkest moment, and finally solves all and wins. It could be a story based on misunderstandings. It could be a story in which the main character, perhaps the only character, has to make a decision. The character's thoughts, questions, and conclusions may be so subtly presented that the reader is scarcely aware of the framework.

With idea and story plan in mind, you still may not be sure of how you're going to tell your story or to whom you want to tell it. So your answer to the question *Are you ready to write?* might be *Not yet.*

IDEA IN A SENTENCE, STORY IN A SENTENCE

What is the foundation idea of your story?

1. Idea
There's this little guy who's tired of a big, strong bully making life miserable for everyone in the neighborhood, so he decides if he can't outfight the bully he'll have to outwit him.

This story idea can be further reduced to fit into the plot/story plan equation.

Character + a complication + what character does about it = story plan

2. Story plan
Pig + Wolf's bullying + how Pig outwits Wolf = story plan

But Numbers 1 and 2 are just the idea and story plan. There are several other things to think about before beginning a story.

Two authors of books on writing, Jane Fitz-Randolph and Barnaby Conrad, agree that before starting, the writer should be able to tell the story in one sentence. They say,

> *In one simple sentence sum up to yourself what the story is about. If you can't do it in one long sentence maybe you have problems; maybe it's not yet clear in your mind.[1]*

—Barnaby Conrad,
*A Complete
Guide to Writing Fiction*

Before you start to write a story—any story—you should write down the whole story in one sentence. Not the story situation, not what the story is about, but the bones, the skeleton, of the whole story. Unless you can do this, either you do not have a story or you have not thought about . . . your material sufficiently to know exactly what story you wish to tell.[2]

—Jane Fitz-Randolph, *How to Write for Children & Young Adults*

Using your idea and story plan, make a story in a sentence. Avoid putting your information together the easy way: ". . . and then . . . and then . . . and then . . .," ending up with a long, compound sentence that is actually several sentences. This story in a sentence will not be the best kind of writing you ordinarily work for, but it will show you the bones of your story.

3. Story in a sentence

The Third Little Pig, seeing the Big Bad Wolf destroy his brothers' houses of sticks and straw, decides to build one of brick, attempting unsuccessfully to discourage the Wolf, who in his efforts to outsmart the Pig, has himself been snared.

WHAT KIND OF FICTION ARE YOU WRITING?

After you concisely state your story, it is time to consider some other details about what you plan to write. Which readers—adults, children, your peers—will be most interested in your story? Are you planning a very short story? A very long story? A novel?

WHO WILL BE YOUR AUDIENCE?

Writing for adults (and that includes publishers' "young adult" category) is writing for people who have already developed interests, opinions, and prejudices. Adult readers bring the dimension of their own experience to what they read, and when writing for them you build on that.

Writing for children involves other considerations. Children's interests and opinions are still forming, and often their first experience in meeting life situations comes in what they read.

Writing for children is not a blanket term. Children are of all ages. Preschoolers and ten-year-olds do not always share the same interests or the same requirements.

Writing for children is not *easier* than writing for adults. It is different. Vocabularies may be simpler but children like new words and strange words. Just be sure that through their use or by explanation they are understandable.

Plots are less involved, and children's stories are much shorter than most stories for adults. That means you will have to learn to use fewer words to express your ideas. Using fewer words means finding the exactly right words—less narrative and more dialogue, less philosophizing and more action.

Adults may have lost the sense of wonder and dreams of adventure they once felt, but these are important elements in writing for children. Perhaps the most important difference in stories for children and stories for adults is that no matter how bleak the situation, stories for children—good stories for children—always carry a spark of hope.

If you would write for children, read what children are reading and, just as when you write for adults, write the very best you can.

HOW LONG WILL YOUR STORY BE?

A novel is an enormous project, taking from months to years to complete. Its length can be anywhere from 25,000 to 150,000 words or longer.

Novellas range in length from that of a long short story to a short novel, 7,500 words to 50,000 words.

Children's books range from a few hundred words (or even fewer in picture books) up to the length of short adult novels. Children's magazine stories, depending on readers' ages, run from 200 words to around 2,000 words. You will find exceptions to all of these figures.

Many different lengths are suggested for adult short stories, usually between 2,000 and 7,000 words; short short stories, 1,000 to 1,500 words; those very short stories called flash or sudden fiction, up to 750 words.

So how long is a short story? Long enough, but just long enough to tell what it is you need to tell.

WHAT IS A SHORT STORY?

And just what is a short story? Edgar Allan Poe described it as a tale "no longer than can be read in a single sitting." Because it is brief, compared to the novel, it must focus sharply on a limited time period and a limited number of characters and happenings. Whether conventional or experimental in its structure, the story has to have something happening. A sketch or vignette can be a still picture of a person or place or of a day. A story has action, physical or mental. A story is about the day in which something different happens to the person or the place, after which nothing will ever be quite the same again.

Jerome Stern in his book *Making Shapely Fiction* says, "Attempts to define the short story seem to be of more interest to critics than to writers," and later adds, "Ultimately, definitions might as well read, 'A short story is what feels like a short story.'"[3]

WHAT KIND OF STORY ARE YOU WRITING?

Look at your story idea and story in a sentence again. Is the main character's problem one of *conflict* or of *decision* or of *discovery*?

Conflict

In this story pattern the character has a specific need, goal, purpose, or wish that he or she must attain, but someone or something is keeping the character from achieving it. There are many kinds of conflicts: physical struggle; conflict of wills, ideas, plans, hopes; or struggles between people with opposing intentions or ambitions.

For the protagonist, the conflict might be a matter of life or death. It could be the attempt to get a job, win a race, or attend the circus. The main character struggles to overcome the opposition and after attempts, failures, and the darkest moment, wins by his or her own courage or ingenuity or special information, training, or talent.

When the conflict is about an unfulfilled wish, there are other ways of solving the problem. Folktales frequently use these patterns. Quoting Jane Fitz-Randolph again,

> *(Wish fulfillment #1) . . . the main character gets his wish because of unselfish or "right" action, done with no thought of getting the wish by this means.*
> *(Wish fulfillment #2, using as an example, the story of Cinderella's wish to attend the ball) . . . in the end Cinderella gets her wish*

and wins the prince, not because of any effort
she makes to go to the ball, but because she
is sweet and forgiving, obedient, and has
small feet.[4]

Decision

In this story pattern the main character must decide what action she will take concerning a problem. It is usually a moral or ethical problem but, whichever decision is made, one that will have an important effect on the main character and probably on others as well.

There may not be a definite antagonist in this type of story—the protagonist might be battling with herself—but there will be others who are affected. The struggle about which way to go reaches a point where the main character must make the (right) decision that the reader is hoping for while fearing it will be the other (wrong) decision.

Discovery

In the story of discovery the main character sees, realizes, comes to understand something that makes a difference in his or her way of thinking or acting or in relationships with others. The discovery may come as a new way of looking at a question, or it could be the straightening out of a misunderstanding. The discovery will be important to the main character, perhaps even life-changing, but the story must not stop there. To be a strong story of discovery, the character will follow the discovery with some action that is a result of the new way of seeing or understanding.

Short stories will use just one or a variation of one of these story patterns. Longer fiction works often use more than one. But whatever the pattern, the story comes into existence with a character who wants or needs something, whose life is in conflict until that something is, one way or another, resolved.

HOW WILL YOU TELL YOUR STORY?

Think of someone telling a group of young children a ghost story. Listen to the storyteller. Now imagine that same person giving a scene from *Macbeth* to an older audience. Hear the difference in the voice, in the style in which the teller presents the material? How you will tell your story depends on

- the type of story
- the audience
- the effect you want
- your own way of seeing and describing

In writing, the word *voice* can mean several different things. It can refer to verb forms: active or passive voice. It is often associated with viewpoint: the first-person voice, the omniscient voice. The term *voice* can also mean the writer's own choice of style, showing through the narrative or through the characters, their thoughts, dialogue, and actions.

The following two paragraphs are about strong-minded cats described in widely different styles. The first is from a story told in a grand, even grandiloquent, way. The second example is a tongue-in-cheek excerpt from a newspaper column.

> . . . *Cat keeps his side of the bargain.* . . . *He will kill mice, and he will be kind to Babies when he is in the house, just as long as they do not pull his tail too hard. But when he has done that, and between times, and when the moon gets up and night comes, he is the Cat*

that walks by himself, and all places are alike to him. Then he goes out to the Wet Wild Woods or up the Wet Wild Trees or on the Wet Wild Roofs, waving his wild tail and walking by his wild lone.[5]

—Rudyard Kipling, "The Cat That Walked by Himself," *Just So Stories*

The only cat I ever knew well was a great yellow beast, name of John L. Sullivan, who lived down near the Navy Yard in southeast Washington. He had a chewed-up nose and two cauliflower ears; he smoked terrible cigars, and he told fearful lies.[6]

—Mike Royko, columnist

The next examples are from two stories of teenage boys with similar problems: they are unhappy with what they believe is the way other people see them. But because of the differences of their backgrounds, they are two quite different boys. Listen to the voice each author gives to his character's thoughts.

I should have been in school that April day.

But instead I was up on the ridge near the old spar mine above our farm, whipping the gray trunk of a rock maple with a dead stick, and hating Edward Thatcher. During recess, he'd pointed at my clothes and made sport of them. Instead of tying into him, I'd turned tail and run off.[7]

—Robert Newton Peck,
A Day No Pigs Would Die

That was my role—the one I seemed born to play. Good Ol' Charlie. The responsible one. The backbone of the world. The one who worked at the refreshment counter while everybody else watched the game. The one who pulled the curtain and did the sound effects for the class play. The one who stayed late and put the chairs away. Good Ol' Charlie.[8]

—P.J. Petersen,
Good-bye to Good Ol' Charlie

Style is how you tell your story. It can mean the way you tell a certain type of story, or it can mean the way in which your characters speak and think. It can mean your own way of saying something. Ralph Waldo Emerson said, "A man's style is his mind's voice." Listen to what you want to say and to how you want to say it. Then decide what your storytelling style and voice will be for each story.

Style is something you develop over time, not something you can install like a computer program.[9]

—Ronald B. Tobias,
Theme & Strategy

DOES YOUR STORY HAVE A THEME?

Theme: the subject about which a person
speaks or writes or thinks.

That is the dictionary definition of theme. There are many more, and each writer or teacher of writing seems to have a definition of his or her own.

Not all stories have obvious or explicit themes. While in some the theme is written out for us, in others we have to search for the theme.

Aesop's fables have a moral or maxim at the end of each story:

"The Boy Who Cried Wolf"	A known liar will not be believed, even when he is speaking the truth.
"The Man, the Boy, and the Donkey"	Please all, and you you will please none.
"The Wolf in Sheep's Clothing"	Appearances are deceptive.

These comments, as well as being spelled-out morals, are the themes of the fables. The theme (or moral, or maxim) for the story of the Three Little Pigs might be, Brains beat brawn, or it could be the same as the moral for the fable of the fox and the stork: One bad turn deserves another. Or if we look at the story from the Wolf's point of view, we could use the moral given for the story of the goose that laid the golden egg: He who wants more often loses all.

Certainly it isn't necessary to point out themes as precisely as the fables do. According to some writers, it may not be important to know just what your theme is before you start to write. Other writers believe it is of prime importance.

Theme . . . is the central concern around which a story is structured. Theme is your . . . guidance system. It directs your decisions about which path to take, which choice is right for the story and which choice isn't.[10]

—Ronald Tobias,
Theme & Strategy

On the other hand,

THEME . . . merely a simple way of defining what you are writing about. . . . My own feeling is that the beginning writer should concentrate on character and conflict and let the themes emerge as they may—and they will, consciously or unconsciously.[11]
—Barnaby Conrad, *The Complete Guide to Writing Fiction*

Lajos Egri, author of *The Art of Dramatic Writing,* prefers the word *premise.* Others, he says, have had different words for the same thing: theme, thesis, root idea, central idea, goal, aim, driving force, subject, purpose, plan, plot, basic emotion.[12] And someone has said that theme is what you remember about a story when you've forgotten the details.

If you know what the theme of your story is, fine. If you don't, you'll no doubt discover it as you work. Leonard Bishop, in *Dare to Be a Great Writer*, says, "After creating a novel the writer should find his theme and claim he knew it all along."[13]

NOW, ARE YOU READY TO WRITE?

A Checklist
1. What is your foundation idea?
2. What is your story-plan equation?
3. What is your story in a sentence?
4. Are you writing a short story, a short short story, or something longer?
5. Is your story one of conflict, of decision, or of discovery?
6. Who is the protagonist? What does he or she want? Why?

7. Is there an antagonist? If so, who is it? What does he or she want? Why?
8. Who are your minor characters? What roles do they play?
9. Where does the story take place?
10. When does the story take place?
11. What role does setting play in your story?
12. From whose viewpoint do you tell the story?
13. Who is your audience?
14. What is the voice in which you tell your story?
15. What is your story's theme?

(You may not be able to answer 13, 14, or 15 until you start writing.)

IS ALL OF THIS NECESSARY?

Is all this preparation necessary? When you're getting ready for a trip, is a map or a travel plan necessary?

Answer to both questions: No, not always, not every time.

If you're going where you've been many times before, then no, you won't need a map. If you have all the time in the world and want to explore country lanes and mountain trails, if you have no destination in mind, then no, you won't need a map.

But if you want to get to a specific place, if you don't want to wander off into dead-end roads, then a map can be a help, even a necessity.

Some writers maintain that when they sit down to start a story they have no idea of where they are going or even what the story will be about. This may work well for some. No doubt some who make this claim don't mention that while they have written no notes, they have thought a great deal about their stories. They also might not mention the number of side roads and blind alleys they occasionally find themselves in.

Experiment. Use all of the steps covered in these first five chapters, use some—or use none. Find out what works best for you. Most important of all, be flexible. No matter how many notes you've made about your antagonist, if, as you write, that antagonist begins to act more like one of the good guys and a minor character becomes villainous, be open to trying them in new roles. If you discover a better setting, experiment with it.

Think about what you want to achieve in your story, where you hope to go, and then choose the best way—the best way for you—to get there.

Now it is time to put your story together.

SIX

TITLES AND BEGINNINGS

The pattern or structure of beginning, middle, and ending for a satisfying story is not something someone devised and then announced: "Hereafter, all stories must fit this pattern." Rather, the structure has developed and come down to us from the time of myths, through folktales, to the present. There is a rhythm to the three parts that satisfies listeners and readers: The beginning catches their attention and makes them curious to know more. The middle adds complications, unexpected happenings, seemingly insurmountable problems, and the ending resolves everything in a satisfactory way.

THE HARDEST STEP IS THAT OVER THE THRESHOLD (JAMES HOWELL'S PROVERBS)

Beginnings are difficult. Taking the first step is difficult. But stories are written one word, one sentence, one paragraph at a time. And remember, those first words can be, no doubt will be, changed, rewritten, thrown away, brought back many times before the story is judged as finished. One word after another, one step after another. It's the only way to get to the place you want to go.

TITLES

THE SIGN ABOVE THE DOOR

Your title is your first chance to grab your reader. It is the sign above the door that invites a customer into the shop. A good title is pertinent and tantalizing. It might be informative. Often it is brief, and almost always it is easy to remember and easy to say.

Study other writers' titles. Look at the books on your shelves. Glance through magazines' tables of contents. Go to the library and to the newsstand and look at more titles. Which ones catch your eye? The subjects you're interested in, of course. But do some of them stop you, even if you're not—you've always thought you were not—interested in the subject?

As you become title-conscious, do you find that some please you because of their rhythm or alliteration? Do some amuse or surprise you with their use of words?

Industries invest fortunes creating packaging for their products, packaging to attract the shopper's attention and make the shopper want to buy. Titles are part of the packaging of your product, the most important promotional feature of your story. So think of the time you spend searching for the perfect title as an investment.

TYPES OF TITLES

Where do titles come from? Everywhere. But most often they come from an idea or even a quotation from the story itself. Maurice Sendak quoted from his story of how Max sailed off through night and day to

Where the Wild Things Are. Although she is long dead before the book begins, the pervading character in Daphne du Maurier's mystery-romance is *Rebecca.*

Another way to find a title is to borrow one. That is not to say you can name a book you plan to write *Gone With the Wind* and have it become a best-seller. Nor is it to say that you should knowingly use other people's titles, although titles cannot be copyrighted. Even without copyright, some titles become so well known that they are considered "properties" and are not for borrowing.

While you're not going to settle for someone else's title, you can find plenty of noncopyrighted quotations to borrow from. The Bible and Shakespeare are the most often used sources for titles; others come from songs, poems, legends, nursery rhymes, and proverbs. Then there is that old standby, Bartlett's *Familiar Quotations.* You don't have to read all of Samuel Johnson in order to quote, "It is only by writing ill that you can attain to write well." There are many other books of quotations besides Bartlett's, so check for them in your library's reference section.

For fiction or nonfiction, short stories or novels, there are five types of titles: labels, statements, questions, imperatives, and combinations of these four. A label title tells what the story is about. It can use one word or a dozen, or more. "Fog" by Carl Sandburg and Judith Viorst's *Alexander and the Terrible, Horrible No Good, Very Bad Day* are labels.

Far less common is the statement title which makes an observation about the subject of the story. Ken Kesey's *One Flew Over the Cuckoo's Nest* and Arnold Lobel's *Frog and Toad Are Friends* are statement titles.

Exclamations show up both in statement titles

and in the remaining title types, questions and imperatives. Imperative titles tell the reader to do something: come, go, look, see, be, do—or better, don't, because the negative has more shock value, is more attention getting. Example: Texas Bix Bender's *Don't Squat With Yer Spurs On*.

You can have fun with title words, using puns (James Howe's *The Celery Stalks at Midnight*), or experimenting with unusual use of words or expressions as John Ciardi does with his book *How Does a Poem Mean?* You can also use alliteration, repetition, and rhyme as in John Steinbeck's *Of Mice and Men*, Conrad Aiken's short story "Silent Snow, Secret Snow," and *Hailstones and Halibut Bones* by Mary O'Neill.

Then there are magic words, certain words that have proved to be special attention-getters: *magic* is one, and *money, mystery, new, secret, success, win,* and *you*. As you read titles, watch for the words that catch your attention. Use them to build your own magic list.

Two more magic words are *How to—*. *Books in Print* lists over thirty pages, approximately 2,500 titles, beginning with *How to—*, and while most of these are nonfiction, the words show up in fiction titles, too.

HOW LONG SHOULD A TITLE BE?

A title should be as long as it takes to do the job. Experts—those who've published enough to have an idea of what works and what doesn't—suggest not more than six words. In a review of recent best-seller lists, most fiction titles were two to four words long, nonfiction titles were three to five words. Robert Fulghum's *All I Really Need to Know I Learned in Kindergarten*, with a ten-word title, was on the best-seller list for months, but his third book, also a best-seller, was titled *Uh-Oh*.

Whatever type of title you choose, whatever length you decide on, keep in mind that memorable titles are usually those that have a hint of rhythm.

The Man Who Would Be King
A River Runs Through It
The Dark Descent

Titles that scan are the easiest to say, and so they are the easiest to remember.

SECOND THOUGHTS

After you have written your story, look at your title again. Does it still fit the story? Has the story taken some unexpected turns since you named it? Have you solved the problem in a different way? Does the title give away the story's ending?

Try the Table of Contents test. Visualize your title in a contents list or on a bookshelf, along with half a dozen or more other titles. Would it catch your eye? Does the sign above the door still represent what is to be found inside the shop?

Your title will be the first thing others read, but it may well be the last part of the story that you write.

BEGINNINGS

A STORY'S BEGINNING

Your story's beginning is your second and last chance to hook your readers. And how do you bait the hook? With suspense! The analogy ends here, because a fisherman can wait hours for his fish. You must catch your readers in the time it takes to read a sentence or two. In fact, Milo O. Frank, communication skills consultant, says, "*The attention span of the average individual is 30 seconds.*"[1] The italics are his.

The suspense to catch your reader doesn't have to be horror-story suspense. It is suspense created by giving your readers some idea of what is going to happen in such an intriguing way that they have to keep reading.

Over and over, editors say that the most common weakness they find in stories is that the stories do not begin at the beginning. Is that double talk? While a novel can afford to be more leisurely, short stories, they tell us, should commence near the middle or even the end of the story. Now that surely is double talk.

The beginning those editors want, that readers want, is the point where something happens. This will be the moment of change, the day that is different, the happening that starts the main character toward the moment of confrontation, or discovery, or decision.

In the opening sentences, readers do not want all the things that occurred and led up to that moment. Hop-along Johnny Doe's troubles may have started with his ancestors or with his first-grade teacher or with the people who owned the ranch before he did, but there is time enough for that information later if it is pertinent to the story. It's the moment when the posse comes thundering into the yard searching for Hop-along that will catch and hold the reader.

Often, in early drafts, writers use several paragraphs or pages of a story to get acquainted with their characters, work out the problem, and find out what kind of a story they are writing. This may serve a very good purpose for some writers, but if you have worked on your character sketches, figured out your plot equation and story in a sentence, and have decided what kind of story it is to be, you don't need to write a first page or chapter that will just be tossed away. You won't waste time writing introductions, you'll jump right in.

SOMETHING HAPPENS

Phyllis A. Whitney says, "Probably tho best way to start any story, long or short, is to show *a character with a problem doing something interesting.*"[2] The problem can be hinted at or stated outright.

> *Aleko became a grave robber mostly out of boredom, though hunger had something to do with it.*[3]
> —John Fischer,
> "A Small Buried Treasure"

> *The thousand injuries of Fortunato I had borne as best I could; but when he ventured upon insult, I vowed revenge.*
> —Edgar Allan Poe,
> "The Cask of Amontillado"

> *One day, as Chicken Licken was walking through the woods, an acorn fell on her head.*
> —Nursery story

The "something interesting" Whitney refers to can be that point at which the main character faces an important change in his or her life.

> *One day The Little Red Hen was scratching in the farmyard when she found a grain of wheat.*
> —Nursery story

EXAMPLE SAMPLES

Stories can begin with one or with a combination of the following:

- Action
- Character
- Dialogue
- Situation
- Setting and mood
- Story theme or philosophical idea

Some writers maintain that action and character openings, especially when combined with dialogue, are the strongest and best attention-getters. The action opening should have a hint, a suggestion of more to come.

> *The small boys came early to the hanging.*[4]
> —Ken Follett,
> *The Pillars of the Earth*

The first sentences of John Gardner's *Nickel Mountain* and E.B. White's *Stuart Little* introduce characters with problem and situation implicit in the descriptions.

> *In December, 1954, Henry Soames would hardly have said his life was just beginning. His heart was bad; business at the Stop-Off had never been worse; he was close to a nervous breakdown.*[5]

> *When Mrs. Frederick C. Little's second son arrived, everybody noticed that he was not much bigger than a mouse. The truth of the*

matter was, the baby looked very much like a mouse in every way. He was only about two inches high; and he had a mouse's sharp nose, a mouse's tail, a mouse's whiskers, and the pleasant shy manners of a mouse.[6]

Although it is not used as often as setting or situation, dialogue openings appeal to our natural inclination to eavesdrop.

"Please, Master," said the cat, "will you change me into a man?"[7]
—Lloyd Alexander,
The Cat Who Wished to Be a Man

A situation opening can indicate action or mood, show something of setting or characters, be heavy with atmosphere, or appear to be a commonplace scene until something uncommon is hinted at or stated.

It was Friday, last period—2:10 p.m.— Senior English. The drone of Mrs. Bethune's nasal twang buzzed, irritating Mark's ears, like a fly he couldn't brush away. He leaned back in his seat, tuning in only enough to answer a question, pass a test, and let his eyes roam across his classmates' backs. Who would it be this time?[8]
—Mary Peace,
Fireflies

It was a bright cold day in April, and the clocks were striking thirteen.[9]
—George Orwell,
1984

The opening that shows setting can be a straight-forward description of a place, but more often it will also introduce characters, show a situation, or create a mood.

> *Fleshless jaws gaped. Hollow eyes streamed seaweed. Atop a cairn of rubble a disembodied skull sat, as if placed there by a macabre prankster, its punctured cranium sporting a dark bryozoan crust that looked like a rakish hat.*[10]
> —Jerry Earl Brown,
> *Under the City of Angels*

The story that begins with its theme or a philo-sophical thought is not likely to have a lot of action in the first few lines, so the opening must be attention-getting in other ways.

> *I am just a business man, not a poet. It is the poet who is supposed to see things so clearly and remember. Perhaps it is only the poets who can die well.*[11]
> —Robert Olen Butler,
> "The Trip Back"

> *There is no delight the equal of dread.*[12]
> —Clive Barker,
> "Dread"

Some stories begin with short sentence grab-bers. Brief as they are, these openings hint at conse-quences.

> *Marley was dead, to begin with.*[13]
> —Charles Dickens,
> *A Christmas Carol*

Last night I dreamt I went to Manderley again.[14]

—Daphne du Maurier,
Rebecca

He came out of the earth hating. Hate was his father; hate was his mother.[15]

—Ray Bradbury,
"Pillar of Fire"

Mom died in the middle of making me a sandwich.[16]

—David Ordan,
"Any Minute Mom Should Come
Blasting Through the Door"

The last camel collapsed at noon.[17]

—Ken Follett,
The Key to Rebecca

Perhaps more than any other technique, the short first sentence must be exactly right. Like a line of poetry . . . every single word counts, and the combination of those few carefully-chosen words is extremely powerful.[18]

—Georgianne Ensign,
Great Beginnings

AFTER THE OPENING

You've caught your reader's attention with your opening sentences. Now get the reader involved, curious, and concerned. When you have the reader's attention, you start filling in details. After the opening, the next paragraphs of the beginning should establish the who, what, when, where, and why of the story as quickly as possible.

WHO

The main character

Establish sex, approximate age, and name here, if you can. This is especially important when the story is told in first person. By action, description, or speech let the reader see what kind of person the main character is.

Now and throughout the story, make sure that your main character *acts* rather than *reacts*. Whenever he or she can, the main character initiates the action while the other characters react to it. A frequently used analogy for this is a tennis game in which the main character always has the serve. The other characters return the ball if or as best they can.

Minor characters

Don't bring all of the other characters onstage at once. Help the reader to get acquainted with them by introducing one or two at a time, by using relationships (Annie's friend, Josie) and personality tags (Annie's giggles, Josie's helpfulness).

Show why these characters are in the story.

For all characters, remember their personality traits and see that their actions are consistent with those traits.

WHAT

Be sure that the problem and why it is a problem to the main character are made clear. Rather than telling about it, show the main character's problem in a scene onstage. Let the reader see firsthand what the character's troubles are about. If there is an antagonist, bring that person, or the threat of that person, onstage, too.

Introduce important clues and information, but do it carefully so as not to give away too much information too early.

WHEN AND WHERE

Begin to fill in background, time, and place. Use specific details and make them sensory. Let your reader smell the new-cut grass or feel the sleet storm or hear the wolves howl.

WHY

Why are all your characters involved? What motivates them? What do they want? It is important to know how they help or hinder the main character, and also to know why they help or hinder.

MORE POINTS TO CONSIDER

Let the readers know the mood of your story as quickly as you can. Is it funny or sad, tragic or heart-warming, mysterious or horrifying? If your title is the sign above the shop door, your beginning paragraphs are the shop window. Be sure that what you display in the window is what you have for sale in your shop.

And now some words of caution. We've talked about grabbing the reader with a dramatic, attention-getting opening.

First, don't let your beginning paragraphs be so dramatic that the rest of the story can't live up to them.

Second, grab your readers, yes, but don't knock them down and stomp on them. Watch that the dramatic doesn't become the melodramatic.

And third, no matter how carefully you've planned your story, as you write you may find your characters doing things you hadn't planned. Very likely you will discover new ideas that give more meaning to what you are saying. Your story may take an unexpected twist that makes it even better.

And when you've finished, what if your original beginning no longer fits the story you have written? What if your beginning no longer points arrow-straight to the ending? You'll rewrite and perhaps rewrite again. Once more you'll write the best beginning you can. And as you do that, keep in mind what the seventeenth-century French philosopher Blaise Pascal said: "The last thing one settles in writing a book is what one should put in first."

SOME THINGS TO THINK ABOUT

Titles and beginnings: Think of them as the start of a chain reaction. Your title catches the notice of a reader. It catches his curiosity. He reads the first line. It catches his attention. He reads the first paragraph. It catches his interest. He reads the first page, turns the page, and your story has caught the reader.

On first reading, a good title will catch a reader's notice, but it may or may not be self-explanatory. Perhaps only after finishing the story will the reader realize, Of course! That is the exactly right title for that story.

> *If you miss the first button-hole, you will not succeed in buttoning up your coat.*
> —Johann Wolfgang von Goethe,
> *Sprache in Prosa*

SEVEN

MIDDLES AND ENDINGS

You're off to a good start. You know where you're going. And to get there, you'll be showing what your main character does about the conflicts and complications he or she faces. You'll be answering the question *How?* How does the protagonist try to solve the problem, and how does the antagonist (or the antagonistic force) try to keep the protagonist from solving the problem? Another *How?* you'll be asking is how to do all of this.

MIDDLES

Conflict is what middles are built of.[1]
—Dwight V. Swain,
"High Middle"

Stories begin with a change in a situation. Change leads to conflict. Whether that means battles with knights on horseback, decisions about how to spend a rainy afternoon, or misunderstandings between friends—physical, mental, or emotional—it is conflict.

Conflict leads to action. Not just knights-in-battle action for the sake of action, but

- action that moves the story along
- action that builds an increasing tension
- action that falls, rises, dips, but overall moves up and up to that darkest moment, to the crisis and climax

Showing what characters do and quoting directly what they say is activity, action. Telling what they did, what they thought, what they had said is, too often, inactivity.

AND THEN . . . AND THEN . . .

For every action there is a reaction; for every move, a countermove.

The First Little Pig built a house of straw. The Wolf blew it down. So the Second Little Pig built a house of sticks. The Wolf blew it down. So the Third Little Pig built a house of bricks. The Wolf could not blow it down, and so thought up other ways to catch the Pig.

Another way of looking at this chain of action is by tracing cause and effect. Cause number one leads to effect number one. In turn, effect number one becomes or is responsible for cause number two.

Because the First Pig built a flimsy house of straw, the Wolf blew it down and ate up the Pig.

Because of the Wolf's actions, the Second Pig built a stronger house of sticks, but

Because the Wolf had succeeded in blowing down the first house, he tried and succeeded in blowing down the second house, and ate up the Pig.

Because the Wolf had blown down the houses of straw and of sticks, the Third Pig built a house of bricks—

With every action or event in your story, look back

for the cause of it. With every action and event, look ahead to find the effect of it. Your characters' actions and reactions will show their strong and weak personality traits and will keep the story moving.

Make sure that one thing leads to another in a logical, or at least an acceptable, fashion. This sequence does not mean cluttering your story with unnecessary details, but rather making the story a strong and believable one. Coincidence and unexplained happenings may be commmon in real life, but there is not room for them in fiction. Stories should have a reason for everything that takes place.

BUILDING SUSPENSE

In chapter 3 we talked about two ways of building suspense to keep your reader reading. Now it is time to put those devices to use.

First, make clear to the reader that there are two possible ways your story can end. There is the ending the reader hopes will happen, but there is also the other ending that the reader hopes will not happen. This dreaded ending should seem far more possible than the hoped-for ending.

Second are the juggling balls of hope, fear, and time. The elements of hope and fear create tension. The action between main character and his opposition creates conflict. Will or won't the character succeed? Add the third element, time, and you build suspense. Will or won't the character succeed—in time?

ONSTAGE

For your readers to believe in the characters' actions, everything those characters need to work with must be put into the story as early as possible.

Think of your story as a play You are the property

manager. The curtain is about to go up. Are all the properties your actors need already on the stage or close at hand in the wings? Properties for your story include objects and settings, talents, knowledge, and abilities.

Does one actor need a piano or a telephone or a car? Let the reader know ahead of time that such properties are available.

Are the distant mountains or the busy city street important? Mention them.

Does Annie have to understand French or Morse code or motorcycle mechanics? Your reader must know about these things before the need for them occurs. And not only must you have all necessary props at hand, every prop and piece of stage scenery should be there for a purpose. It will be there either to help develop your characters or to move the plot along.

If your story opens with the description of a spec-tacular sunset, that sunset can't just be decoration. There must be a reason for it. Perhaps it affects the main character's mood. Perhaps it is symbolic, the end of something. It might be a time marker, the story moving from one sunset to the next. Or a time limit: It is now sunset and something must be accomplished before sunrise—or before dark!

The sunset would be a part of that suspense-builder you catch your reader with.

MORE DEVICES

For other ways of holding the reader's attention, try some of the storyteller's techniques.

First there is the magic of three's. Think how often we use them:

- Life, liberty, and the pursuit of happiness
- First, last, and always

- Faith, hope, and love
- Tom, Dick, and Harry

We started out when very young with three blind mice, three billy goats Gruff, three little kittens. We went on to tales of kings with three beautiful daughters and woodcutters with three sons who went out into the world to seek their fortunes. They were given three tasks to perform, three riddles to solve, they were granted three wishes.

Use three's in your plotting. Give your hero three chances to solve the problem. With the first two attempts, bring this character closer to that darkest moment and the ending your reader fears will happen. Then, with the third attempt, when all seems lost, have the hero make the right choice or the right discovery or the right maneuver to find success.

Three characters can be a friendly trio or they can be a feuding triangle. Three's can be very satisfying, even in conflict, so put them to work for you.

Pacing is another of the storyteller's devices. In moments of action, shorten sentences and use words that are brief and quick. This speeds up action and helps to build tension and excitement. You bring your reader up close, right into what is happening. You create immediacy.

The knights were surging up around her. Hoofs battered on the ground. All around her were the heavy mailed bodies of the men and their plunging horses. Somewhere people were screeching. Maria's horse reared, flailing out with its hoofs. An arrow jutted from its neck, fletched with red feathers.[2]

—Cecelia Holland,
Great Maria

Long words and long sentences slow action. Slowing down will give your readers, and your characters, a release from intense emotion and a moment to catch their breath before the action starts up again. It can also distance your readers, show a broader picture, and create a somber or thoughtful or mysterious mood.

> *During the whole of a dull, dark, and soundless day in the autumn of the year, when the clouds hung oppressively low in the heavens, I had been passing alone, on horseback, through a singularly dreary tract of country; and at length found myself, as the shades of evening drew on, within view of the melancholy House of Usher.*
>
> —Edgar Allan Poe,
> *The Fall of the House of Usher*

The selection from *Great Maria* has forty-nine words divided into six sentences. The longest word, *Maria*, has three syllables.

The opening for *The Fall of the House of Usher* has fifty-nine words. Poe's percentage of short words is greater than Holland's, but so is his percentage of long words. Poe's total fifty-nine words make up just one sentence. The word and sentence lengths are important in developing the widely different spirit of these two examples, but equally important are the words and phrases the authors chose.

For action, use quick, strong verbs; active voice; short, vivid nouns and adjectives; and short sentences. For reflective or foreboding moods or for a pause and rest after high action, change your pace. Choose quiet words, words that take longer to say, and an occasional passive-voice verb.

THOSE THREE WORDS AGAIN

Now let's go back to the writer's three magic words:

SHOW, DON'T TELL

In chapter 4 we talked about showing settings. Now we'll look at ways to show other things.
If you read,

Kevin was angry when he struck out,

all you can do is take the writer's word for it. All you know is that Kevin is angry. But if you read,

When Kevin struck out, he threw down his bat, kicked the umpire, and stomped back to the bench,

then you see Kevin. You see how he acts when he's angry or upset. And so you know something about Kevin.

When Josh strikes out, he bites his lip and goes off by himself for a while. And when Seth strikes out, he bursts into tears. By seeing how they act, you learn a little about these boys, and later on in the story, when something else upsetting happens, you have some idea as to how each will react.

It isn't always necessary that your readers visualize exactly as you do, but if you are trying to make a precise picture, then find precise words. Go from the general to the specific.

The man walked down the street.

What kind of man? Was he old, young, the mayor, a

stranger? How did he walk? Did he move quickly or slowly? Did he limp? What kind of street? Was it a busy street, a tree-shaded road, or a dusty country lane?

Even the terms *old man* or *walked slowly* may not be specific enough to make the picture you want. One thesaurus gives nine different words meaning *old man*, over fifty words illustrating different ways of walking, thirty-five words that mean to *move slowly*, and almost sixty terms for road or street.

Even if we say,

> *The old man dressed in red walked slowly*
> *down the street,*

each reader will see a different man and a different street. It might be a white-haired gentleman wearing a maroon blazer or a mysterious stranger in scarlet cloak and pantaloons. Or it might be Santa Claus.

As you write, hunt for a few best words instead of lots of rather good words. Try to avoid the general word. *Walked* doesn't give as clear a picture as *strolled*. Sometimes, though, just one word isn't enough. *Lane* might be more exact than *street*, but *winding, tree-shaded lane* could be the picture you want.

A few carefully chosen words can create a whole picture. *The girl wore a coat* tells a fact. A brief description of the coat shows a picture of the girl:

> *The girl wore a full-length mink coat.*
> *The girl wore a studded, black-leather jacket.*
> *The girl wore a too-large raincoat, dirty and torn.*

Use adjectives and adverbs if they are needed, but remember that more is not necessarily better.

> *Bright silvery moonlight was shining down*
> *on the little town.*

Ten words.

Moonlight silvered the village.

Same picture in four words.

Look for the verb or the noun that can do the job without leaning on adverbs and adjectives.

Opinion words can be lazy, nothing words, too. To say *Josie is happy* or *Kevin is angry* is to make a judgment, to give an opinion. It is telling your reader what to think. Sometimes *angry, happy, nice, good, very*, or *great* are the exact words to do the job, but often they don't tell enough to show a picture. Show, don't tell. You can't *see* nice.

MIDDLES MEAN COMPLICATIONS

Whenever and wherever it is possible, show the complications of your story plan by action and dialogue. These episodes of action and dialogue are called scenes. Each scene is like a mini-story with a setting in which characters, by trying to achieve their various purposes, are creating conflict. The scene will reach a crisis point, which may or may not be resolved. If the immediate conflict is not resolved, it adds to the main character's problems. If it is resolved, it leads to more conflicts. (Because . . . because . . .)

As with the story, the scene also begins with something happening. Explanations can come later. And as in the entire story, everything in the scene must be there to move the story along. If characters discuss the weather, it is not because they are making conversation, but because the weather has a place in the story plan.

The action of the scene can help to develop the mood of the story, show the attitudes and motivations of the characters, and hint at things to come.

The scene ends with the main character in more of a quandary, in more difficulty than before. It also ends with a hook to keep the reader asking, What next?

During a scene the reader is onstage with the actors. The reader will see the scene. So as you plan it, you, too, must be onstage watching and listening to everything your characters do and say. You must see, if your readers are to see.

EXPOSITION AND NARRATION

Those are intimidating terms, exposition and narration. A narrative is a story. Narration is the telling of a story, of what happened. Exposition is merely explaining things.

A certain amount of explaining is necessary in the course of a story. A character can give some of this, or it can be given through the thoughts of the viewpoint character. But sometimes the writer has to give the information, and in doing this, the writer must avoid author intrusion.

In the past, writers often came into the story to say, "And now, dear reader, I must explain . . ." or "Poor Dora would never know what happened on that fateful day." Once the play has started, the stage manager does not join the actors onstage.

SOMETIMES IT'S TELL, DON'T SHOW

Narration *tells*.

Sometimes it takes too long, too many words, to show what can be told in a sentence or two. Some events are necessary to the story but not very exciting. In these places, summarize. Tell, don't show.

Narration can
- establish setting and mood
- help to characterize
- describe complications
- review what has happened in a previous scene
- build interest and suspense for the next scene.

Kari thought over what the detective had told her. He'd been grumpy about it, but if he was right, she had nothing more to worry about. Unless . . .

Narration is also used as a bridge from one time to another, one place to another, one character to another, one viewpoint to another. These bridges are called transitions.

Transitions can be a few words or several sentences.

Time:	An hour later— The next day—
Place:	The village had been cool and quiet, but the city was noisy and hot.
Person:	Bill was standing at the bus stop when the siren sounded. Across town, Meg heard the siren just as she was locking the house door.
Viewpoint:	Pig didn't believe for one minute that Wolf had thought at all about the weather. But Wolf had given the weather a great deal of thought.

A transition that moves the story from one person or one viewpoint to another can be done only in multiple-viewpoint or omniscient-viewpoint stories.

Transitions slow the story pace. While this gives the reader a brief rest from the action, narration for any purpose should not be too long and detailed, and it should always keep the story moving.

FLASHBACKS

Another kind of transition takes the story back in time through a flashback. Usually something sensory evokes a memory; that remembered incident is then played onstage with dialogue and action. Flashbacks are not often used in short stories. They don't merely slow action, they bring it, for a time, to a complete stop. Instead of flashbacks, an event is remembered and told by a character or thought about by the viewpoint character.

When using transitions that move from one character to another, or into and out of flashbacks, you need to be especially clear about the change of person, time, or place. After a flashback, pick up the character in the same spot as before the flashback.

ENDINGS

THE MOMENT OF DECISION

All this showing and telling, explanation and action, moves the middle of the story to the darkest moment. This is the high point of suspense for the reader, but for the main character it is the low point of the experience.

At the darkest moment all seems lost. The main character, after self-examination, must face his or her weakest trait. It is do-or-die, succeed-or-fail time. This turning point is the moment of crisis and climax.

(Many writers use the terms interchangeably, others differentiate—crisis first, then climax.)

It is too late to sit down and think about the problem. The protagonist must act, based on emotions now, not logic. And will whatever the protagonist is feeling be what is right? The reader hopes so, because it is the ability to face hardship or danger, to make a sacrifice in the moment of crisis, that turns an ordinary character into a hero.

The main character's struggle with decision is called an obligatory scene. It is not to be skipped over or reduced to telling about. It must be played onstage for the reader to see, hear, and take part in.

WHEN IT'S TIME, SAY GOOD-BYE AND GO

You've done everything you can to make a good, strong story. The protagonist has made a decision, done something in the light of a discovery, banished the antagonist or at least helped the antagonist to recognize his or her errors. You've reached the logical ending. Logical and believable, but not predictable. As they near the ending, your readers may guess what is going to happen but should not be able to guess how it is going to happen.

The best beginning in the world will not guarantee a satisfactory ending. Know where you are going, even if, when you start, you're not sure how you are going to get there.

- Don't count on an ending simply to show up.
- Don't try to sneak in last-minute new characters or stage props to get you off the hook.
- Don't avoid the details of resolving your story by writing, "And then I woke up. It was all a dream." That worked for Lewis Carroll but it doesn't work for every writer.
- Don't tell your readers what they should think or

feel at the end of your story. In fact, don't ever tell your readers what to feel. Show what the character feels, and let the readers make up their own minds as to how they feel.

• And never depend on last-minute miracles, either for your characters or for you.

THE SATISFACTORY ENDING

In fiction, the right ending is not necessarily the happiest ending, but to be a strong ending it should show change in the main character.

Action in a story does not have to be physical action. A more subtle action is the change in a character through dealing with problems. In a downbeat story the change might be deterioration, but a character who grows and benefits from experience is more interesting and more believable than the character who learns nothing.

An ending doesn't have to be a twenty-one-gun salute, but it should be at least as emphatic and memorable as the beginning. Your ending will give readers their last—and lasting—feelings about your story.

Tie up loose ends. Not everything has to be worked out and finished off completely, but don't leave Grandma and Rover locked in the closet.

Beware of a meandering ending that lets the point of your story fade away. Make your final sentences short and strong, but don't let the last paragraphs be so abrupt that the reader is not sure what happened and turns the page thinking there must be a little more. Give the reader some time to enjoy the way things did, after all, work out before you shut the door. And when you do close the door, don't slam it.

In *The Way to Write for Children*, Joan Aiken tells

how her daughter, a fan of C. S. Lewis's Narnia books, wrote to the author to ask what happened after the last one, how the story really ended. Lewis's answer was that he didn't know the end because it hadn't happened yet.[3]

So leave a few things for the reader to think about. Leave enough to let your characters and your story go on living in the reader's imagination.

In Shakespeare's *A Winter's Tale*, after Antigonus finishes his long speech, the stage directions for him are, *Exit, followed by a bear.*

SOME THINGS TO THINK ABOUT

Give narrative immediacy by showing the character, even though you are telling about what the character does.

Not this,

As he went up the steps, Joe heard the clock strike the hour.

But this,

Joe took the steps two at a time as the tower clock chimed five.

Just sitting and worrying is not action. The hero worries, of course, but worries while doing something, successful or unsuccessful, about the problem.

To touch your readers' emotions, zero in. Show them one face in the crowd, one stray dog. In a battle scene, don't picture the whole army. Robert Newton Peck says, "A writer must see one soldier, with one musket, during one moment in his young life."[4]

EIGHT

LET'S TALK ABOUT TALK

Dialogue, more than anything else, increases a book's readability. Readers have an easier and more enjoyable time with those books in which the characters do a lot of talking to one another than those in which the author spends all his time telling what's happening.[1]
—Lawrence Block,
Writing the Novel

You can *tell* what happens by using narrative. The scene you write with dialogue will *show* the action and reaction of the characters, give quick characterizations, and bring life and immediacy to a story.

REAL TALK? OR TALK THAT SOUNDS REAL?

Be an eavesdropper. Listen to what people say and, especially, to how they say it. Watch them as they talk. Some people speak like textbooks. Most don't. Most of us don't speak in complete sentences. We say *uh* and *mmm*, *oh* and *well*. We punctuate with *you know* and *I mean*.

Hear what people say, but when you write dialogue, don't duplicate what they say. Rather than reproduce real conversation, which can ramble and repeat, imitate the artist who draws an impression of a tree with three pencil strokes or a person's profile with a curvy line and a dot.

Hear, too, how people say what they say. Do they talk in questions that they don't expect answers for? Do they talk in clichés? Do they interrupt and change the subject? Do they always yell when they're angry?

What you write will sound like what people say, but it will be condensed, it will contain the spirit of real conversations without the load of extra words and meanderings. One "uh" or "you know" on the page will be enough to give your reader an idea of the person speaking. Study your character charts and biographies. Would this character say "My friend and I" or would he say "Me and another guy?"

A person's speech reveals

- education
- intelligence
- ethnic and geographical background
- character traits

Know your characters, then let them speak for themselves in their own individual voices. They might think in figures of speech, but when they talk, they probably will use ordinary generalities. If Joe asks Annie, "How's the weather?" she is more likely to answer, "Oh, it's cold," than to copy a poet and say, "Oh, the crisp white snow has a soda-cracker crunch."

GOOD DIALOGUE TELLS MORE THAN IT SAYS

Story conversation isn't just he said–she said—isn't just chatter. Good dialogue has many jobs to do. It won't take the place of narrative and exposition, but it does give information. This is not the, "Well, here we are in Saint Louis at the 1904 Louisiana Purchase Centennial Exposition" kind of information, but information that keeps the characters and story plan alive and going.

Conversation between characters can establish relationships:

"Well, well, well," said the Wicked Wolf, "if it isn't my friend, Little Red Riding Hood."

It can ask for information:

"And where are you going with that nice basket of goodies?"

It can give information:

"I'm going to my grandmother's house," Little Red Riding Hood replied.

Dialogue can keep the story from slowing down for a lengthy flashback by having someone say, "Do you remember . . ." It can foreshadow: "I told him it's a crazy idea and it'll never work." It can show something about the character, and at the same time give story background information and help to establish mood and setting.

"No way am I going down that street, not after dark I'm not. Listen, I get cold chills just going by that house in daylight. You don't believe me that it's haunted? Well, there was this woman . . ."

Characters counter questions with more questions or skip ahead and answer questions not yet asked.

Miranda Doe serves Hop-Along Johnny Doe some steak for dinner. Hop-Along asks, "Where did you get this steak?" Miranda Doe answers, "At the ABC Meat Market. Here, have some more Brussels sprouts."

End of scene.

But if Hop-Along asks, "Where did you get this steak?" and Miranda Doe answers, "What's wrong with it?" the scene is just beginning.

Stimulus and response. Action and reaction. Give and take. Show the important parts of the story with dialogue and action. Tell about the less important parts with narrative.

THAT FOUR-LETTER WORD *SAID*

There is nothing wrong with the word *said*. It is a word the eye slides over, just as the eye slides over commas and periods. If your characters are well drawn, your reader will usually know who is speaking, so not every speech will have to carry a name tag. This is especially true when two characters are speaking. Just use enough identification so that the reader doesn't have to count back to be sure who is saying what.

If only two are speaking and you write, "Have some pizza, Annie," there is no need to add *said Joe*. And remember that people don't use names a great deal in direct conversation. Too much identification begins to sound ridiculous.

"Thank you for the pizza, Joe."
"You're welcome, Annie."
"But, Joe, you may have the anchovies."
"Thank you, Annie."
"You're welcome, Joe."

The words the eye does not slide over are those descriptive verbs such as he *affirmed*, she *avowed*, he *intoned*, she *quipped*. Let what the character says indicate how she says it.

If Josie's words are "Help! I'm drowning!" is it necessary to add *she exclaimed*?

SPEAKING ADVERBIALLY

If it is important for Josie to exclaim whatever she has to say, certainly she does not need to exclaim *excitedly*. Play the Tom Swifty game, and you'll think twice about overuse of adverbs.

- "I never loaf," the baker said crustily.
- "You'll have to wait your turn," the barber said cuttingly.
- "The cemetery gates are locked," the sexton said gravely.
- "I can't find them anywhere," Little Bo Peep said sheepishly.

OTHER WAYS TO SPEAK

Use words other than *said* when they are important to the meaning—*whispered, shouted*, and, *yes, exclaimed*. But be sure the verb fits the words. Hissing is for words with the letter S. Perhaps someone could hiss, "Listen, Josie!" but not "Mother, come here." And does your character really rasp or growl? A paperback romance had the macho hero rasping all his speeches. At the obligatory moment, he even rasped, "I love you."

Nor would that hero have been able to laugh or smile, "I love you." Let your characters laugh and then speak or speak and then laugh.

So you'll use the word *said*. But where do you put

it? It doesn't always have to be at the end of the sentence.

> *Josie said, "I'll go."*
> *"I'll go," Josie said, "if you want me to."*

Sometimes you don't have to use it at all.

> *"I'll go." Josie started to the door, then paused. "That is, if you want me to."*

Be sure to find the natural place for the break.

Not, "I'm," Josie said, "going now," unless Josie did pause before finishing her sentence.

> *"I'm—" Josie paused, "I'm going now."*

If in doubt, find the natural place for the break by reading the speech aloud.

Change the pattern occasionally, not only for variety, but also for emphasis. A workshop teacher once said, "If the first words of a sentence, any sentence, not just dialogue, are worth five dollars, then the last words of a sentence are worth ten dollars. And the words in between are worth thirty-nine cents."

This advice is not for every sentence, but do be aware of which parts of a sentence are most important.

DIRECT OR INDIRECT QUOTATIONS

Dialogue can be presented in three ways. First is the direct quotation:

> *"I'm going to my grandmother's house. She's sick and I am taking her this basket of goodies."*

Second is the indirect quotation:

Little Red Riding Hood said she was going to her grandmother's house, that she was taking a basket of goodies because her grandmother was sick.

Third is the brief summary:

Little Red Riding Hood told the Wolf she was on her way to her grandmother's house.

If the information is important enough to include, but not important enough for a scene with conversation and action, the dialogue can be given indirectly or in summary.

DOES YOUR READER HEAR AND SEE AS YOU DO?

Just as much as the words characters say, how they say them will show those characters to the reader. Readers will supply their own expression and inflection to dialogue if you don't do it for them. In this sample question, *Why did you go to Riverville?*, what is it that the questioner wants to know?

- *Why* did you go to Riverville?
- Why did *you* go to Riverville?
- Why did you go to *Riverville?*

You can use italics to make sure the reader understands:

Why did you go to Riverville?

You might add some explanation:

Joe couldn't see Annie doing anything she could get someone else to do, so he asked, "Why did you go to Riverville?"

Or, you might rewrite the sentence:

"Why, of all places, did you go to Riverville?"

One way to indicate how a character speaks is to establish feelings or attitude first.

Annie glanced at the invitation and shrugged. "Riverville. I guess I'll go."

We see Josie's behavior before she speaks. We have no need to add, *she said indifferently.*

What a character does while speaking can give to or take away from the importance of the words or the situation.

"Chickens?" said Dirk. "What chickens?"

"Well, apparently," said Kate, lowering her voice and leaning forward a little, "he's always having live chickens delivered to his hotel room."

Dirk frowned.

"What on earth for?" he said.

"Nobody knows. Nobody ever knows what happens to them. Nobody ever sees them again. Not," she said, leaning even farther forward, and dropping her voice still lower, "a single feather."[2]

—Douglas Adams,
*The Long Dark Tea-time
of the Soul*

Suppose, instead of leaning forward and lowering her voice, Kate had leaned back and let her gaze wander around the room, or she had taken a mirror from her handbag and checked her mascara. We would know then, her words to Dirk to the contrary, that she really wasn't much interested in the chickens. Or if she had smiled in a sly or meaningful way as she had said, "Nobody knows," we would understand that she meant *Nobody—but Kate.*

If what the character does contradicts her words, you'll have even more tension building in your story.

SLANG AND DIALECT

In writing dialogue, a small amount of slang or trendy expressions can add flavor, but it can also date your story. Use timeless expressions or make up your own.

As to dialect and phonetic spelling, be careful. Overdoing it can make your character sound like a parody. Your reader may find reading it like translating a foreign language. It is safer to imply the way of speaking by cadence, regional expressions, or sentence structure.

Rather than trying to imitate an accent, *Theese eeze eet?,* hint at a different sentence structure or inflection, *It is this, no?*

As an identification tag, your characters might once or twice say *gonna, y'all*, or drop a final *g*. For the flavor of speech other than English, add an easily translatable word or two of the language. A few hints go a long way.

One line of dialogue can have more impact than a paragraph of narrative or exposition. It can, unobtrusively

- explain a situation
- establish a mood
- build suspense
- show attitudes
- allow insight into a character
- bring a touch of humor

and, perhaps most important of all, dialogue can show action and interplay among characters as it moves the story along.

SOME THINGS TO THINK ABOUT

Keep your reader aware not only of how a speech is said but also of how it is received.

Look critically at any character's speech that goes on for longer than three lines.

Characters should speak in their own voice, in their own way, not in the author's voice or the author's way.

"And what is the use of a book," thought Alice, "without pictures or conversation?"

NINE

TIPS AND TECHNIQUES

Writing is communicating. When you share your thoughts and ideas you must give them a fair chance—no, *the best advantage*—so that when they reach your reader they will say exactly what you mean.

Think of your readers as out for an evening's stroll. Will they stub their toes on a misplaced pronoun or modifier? Will they have to dodge dangling participles or retrace their steps because of awkward constructions? Unfortunately, your readers are under no obligation to stay with you. They may decide the stroll isn't worth the effort. When you speak face-to-face, you see if you are losing your audience. You may not know if it is from their *not* understanding, *mis*understanding, or boredom, but you see yawns and fidgets, and you do something about them. With writing, you can only put yourself in your reader's place: How would this sound if I were reading it for the first time? What would it mean to me?

SENTENCES

A sentence names something and expresses a complete thought about what it has named.

A sentence has two parts: *what*, the subject, and *what about*, the predicate. A sentence can give merely subject and verb with no descriptive words. *Bees fly. Years pass.* But many sentences give additional information to the what and what about. These sentences can also be divided into three parts: beginning, middle, and ending, and each part has a function.

As with the beginning of a story, a chapter, or a paragraph, the beginning of a sentence should catch attention. The middle of the sentence gives information and details. The last words tell readers what is most important for them to remember.

When you're eating a sandwich, the chicken or cheese may be more important to you than the top and bottom slices of rye. But when you write a sentence, the middle is not as important as what is on either side. Remember the dollar value put on a sentence?

Beginning — $5
Middle — 39¢
End — $10

If we write,

When Little Red Riding Hood met the Wolf, she was hurrying through the woods,

it is all right to give the heroine the $5 place, although she doesn't have to be there in every sentence. But which is more important to the story, the hurrying or the Wolf? Let's rearrange the sentence:

Little Red Riding Hood $5
was hurrying through the woods 39¢
when she met the Wolf $10

When you have written a good sentence, stop. Afterthoughts can spoil the effect.

Little Red Riding Hood's mother never should have sent her little girl through the woods alone, it seems to me.

Why trade a ten-dollar ending for a postscript of no value?

Placement is also important in listing words or phrases in a sentence. The most important word or phrase comes last, and if all are of equal importance, the longest one comes last.

The woodcutter was honored with a medal from the Mayor, cookies from Grandma, and a kiss from Little Red Riding Hood.

Usually the dollar-value arrangement will make the strongest sentences, but there are times when you will want to establish necessary information first. "I'm falling—help!" is not as effective as "Help! I'm falling—"

At times, first place should go to action before speech or thought. The following sentence gives Grandma's reaction before it gives her action, although it is all right to leave the surprise of the Wolf until the last.

Grandma got the fright of her life when she looked up and saw the Wolf.

Now let's show what happens, as it happens:

Grandma looked up and got the fright of her life—there stood the Wolf!

TO BE OR NOT TO BE

The sentence above could have ended, there was the Wolf!, but it would not have been as strong a sentence. Forms of the verb *to be* just sit there, being.

To show, not tell, try other verbs before settling for a form of to be,

Ms. Pumpkin-Eater is in the pumpkin shell.
Ms. Pumpkin-Eater lives (stays, hides, sulks, entertains) in the pumpkin shell.
The sheep are in the meadow, and the cows are in the corn.
The sheep grazed in the meadow, while the cows trampled the corn.

If they are the right ones for your sentence, use *to be* verbs: "Now is the time for all good men . . ." "To be or not to be . . ."

ACTIVE OR PASSIVE?

Did the Little Red Hen plant the wheat, or was the wheat planted by the Little Red Hen?

Active voice: subject is doer of the action
Passive voice: subject is receiver of the action
active: moving about, energetic, busy
passive: submissive, acted upon, uninvolved

Notice that *energetic* is a synonym for active. Active verbs show things happening, moving, progressing. Active-voice sentences usually are stronger than passive-voice sentences, but there are times to use passive verbs.

- When the action and receiver are more important than the doer:

The King was crowned.

- When the doer is unknown, or when you want to keep the doer unknown:

The King's crown was stolen.

- When you want to show the subject as a submissive or acted-upon person:

Ms. Pumpkin-Eater was tricked by her husband Peter.

PROBLEM SENTENCES

Ungrammatical constructions can make readers stub a toe or fall flat on their face. A few CAUTION—ROUGH ROAD AHEAD warnings for you may help to protect you and your readers.

RIDING MY BICYCLE, A DOG ALMOST BIT ME

Beware of and be aware of dangling phrases and clauses. A dangler is a modifier that seems to be modifying the wrong thing or that is left hanging with nothing to modify.

We saw the flowers walking in the garden.
While walking in the garden, we saw the flowers.

If we leave out or imply the subject or verb of a clause, we might forget what we are talking about.

> *When still a puppy, I taught Fido to shake hands.*
> *When he was still a puppy, I taught Fido to shake hands.*

or

> *When still a puppy, Fido learned to shake hands.*

Danglers can slip in anywhere, but they seem to cause the most trouble at the beginning of sentences. Often, changing the sentence order or adding a few words will take care of the problem.

> *A dog almost bit me when I was riding my bicycle.*
> *When I was riding my bicycle, a dog almost bit me.*

THE DOG BIT MY TIRE AND THEN IT SPRANG A LEAK

Watch for orphaned pronouns. True, the pronoun *it* is closer to the word *tire* than it is to *dog*. But the phrase *and then* makes *it* seem to refer to *dog*.

> *My tire sprang a leak when the dog bit it.*

LATER I SAW THE DOG WITH A GIRL ON A LONG LEASH.

When modifiers wander too far from where they belong, the results can be confusing, amusing, or at any rate distracting.

LATER, I SAW A GIRL WITH THE DOG ON A LONG LEASH

You will find rules about danglers and misplaced modifiers in grammar or style and usage books, but you can catch most awkward and ridiculous constructions by reading your sentences aloud and listening as you read.

SENTENCES WITH TOO MANY WORDS

When sentences seem too long, check them for unnecessary words.

- Are openers such as *There are, It is, In order to*, necessary for the meaning?

There are five things that are important to remember.
Five things are important to remember.

- *Are nouns trying to do a verb's job?*

"I have made the decision to plant the wheat," the Little Red Hen said, carrying out the implementation of her plan.
"I have decided to plant the wheat," the Little Red Hen said, and she did.

- Are some of the words saying the same thing twice?

first began	final conclusion
small trifle	consensus of opinion
free gift	carry out the implementation

- Are all of the adverbs necessary?

walked slowly—strolled, ambled
walked slowly and tiredly—trudged, plodded
walked unsteadily—staggered, limped,
hobbled

- Are nothing words—modifiers that don't show anything and tell too little—creeping in?

neat guy   *good* party   *nice* day

RHYTHM ISN'T JUST FOR POETRY

Good writing has a restrained rhythm, a cadence that makes the words easy to read and often easy to remember. The rhythm is created by a recurring sequence or pattern. Sometimes a repetition of words makes the pattern ("It was the best of times, it was the worst of times . . .").

Sometimes the rhythm is created by the words themselves, not the obvious ta-dum ta-dum ta-dumpity-dum of a drumbeat, but a subtle balance of phrases and words.

Lightning twitched like a dreaming dog's legs. The wind blew. Rain fell. And Zorelli lay awake in the night.[1]

—Paul Fleischman,
"The Man of Influence"

Repetitions of sounds, words, and phrases are common in folktales and nursery stories and rhymes.

"Little pig, little pig, let me come in."
"No, no, by the hair of my chinny chin chin."

You'll find frequent use of repetitions in Shakespeare's works and in the Bible.

> *I had an Edward, till a Richard kill'd him;*
> *I had a Harry, till a Richard kill'd him;*
> *Thou hadst an Edward, till a Richard kill'd him;*
> *Thou hadst a Richard, till a Richard kill'd him.*
> —*King Richard III*

Alliteration creates rhythm, but use it sparingly because it can be distracting. Too many repeated sounds will make readers think of "Peter Piper" and "She Sells Seashells."

Two of the most effective devices in writing are *parallelism* and *antithesis*. Parallel structure puts ideas—words, phrases, clauses—of equal importance into the same grammatical form and, in doing so, creates rhythm.

not	tall, dark, and being good looking
but	tall, dark, and handsome
not	Old King Cole called for his pipe, servants brought his bowl, and he told his fiddlers to come.
but	Old King Cole called for his pipe, called for his bowl, and called for his fiddlers three.

Antithesis uses parallel construction to contrast ideas, as in the earlier-quoted opening of *A Tale of Two Cities* by Charles Dickens.

> *It was the best of times, it was the worst of times . . .*

124

In the second paragraph Dickens continues,

There were a king with a large jaw and a queen with a plain face, on the throne of England; there were a king with a large jaw and a queen with a fair face, on the throne of France.

Write, then read aloud, and listen. To quote James J. Kilpatrick, author of *The Writer's Art,* "One must listen to the sound of one's own prose. If a sentence lacks cadence, the sentence collapses like an overcooked soufflé."[2]

WORDS

Mark Twain said, "I never write 'metropolis' for seven cents when I can get the same price for 'city.'" Some readers may have a vocabulary the size of a dictionary, but for the most part, the words that will keep them reading are the concrete rather than the abstract, the short rather than the long. Short words are more vigorous than long words, and they usually are more familiar. *Expeditiousness engenders profligateness* misses the precise meaning and lacks the punch of *Haste makes waste.*

It is not unkind to send your reader to the dictionary once in a while, but it is better if you can make the meaning of a strange word understandable by the way you use it. Nor is it wrong for you to go to the dictionary or thesaurus to find the exact word for the occasion. Just be sure you aren't sending a white-tie-and-tails word to a square dance.

WORD PICTURES

Figures of speech are more than mere decorations for writing. They add color and

*imagery, and they imply more than the words
actually say. They change abstract ideas into
experiences and pictures we can relate to.*[3]
—Kathleen C. Phillips and
Barbara Steiner,
Catching Ideas

Among the most frequently used figures of speech are

- simile
- metaphor
- personification
- hyperbole

A *simile* says something is like or similar to something else.

*Like silent, hungry sharks that swim in the
darkness of the sea, the German submarines
arrived in the middle of the night.*[4]
—Theodore Taylor,
The Cay

*Mrs. Dagget was big as a skinned ox . . .
she was holding a three-pronged candle
holder like it was the Devil's own pitchfork.*[5]
—Sid Fleischman,
Jingo Django

A *metaphor* says something is something else. It points out or implies what the two have in common.

In chapter 2 we used the comparison game to develop character personalities.

Mrs. Biddle is a chickadee.
Bert is a Chevy pickup.

These comparisons are metaphors. Develop such metaphors for more detailed and vivid pictures.

Mrs. Biddle is a chickadee of a person—hopping, chirping, busy, busy, busy.
On the outside he was a Chevy pickup, but inside, Bert knew he had been born a Firebird.

William Mayne, in his book *Sand*, uses both metaphor and simile to describe a boy's trying to get dressed in a frigid room.

The shirt was made of cold cloth and frozen buttons.
It lay on Ainsley's bed like a drift of snow.
It had been starched with ice.[6]

Personification gives human characteristics to objects or abstract ideas.

The arch of aspen . . . flailed and slapped at us. Almost bare, the branches reached out greedily, teasing and tearing at our cloaks.[7]
—Alix Ainsley,
The House of
Whispering Aspens

Hyperbole is a form of exaggeration used for special effects.

Dogtown was a lumpy checkerboard of small homes, blocks of overcrowded flats, and alleys that even scavenging rats entered only in pairs. . . .
As for the rats, they were so fierce that they

*were said to have hijacked garbage trucks
and left the crews bound and gagged.*[8]

—Frank Bonham,
Mystery of the Fat Cat

Although figures of speech include more devices than the four mentioned here, the word *metaphor* is often used to mean any such word picture.

Figures of speech help us, as writers, to illustrate and make our points effectively.

Figures of speech help us, as readers, to see and think about things in ways we hadn't seen or thought about before.

Theodore M. Bernstein, author of *The Careful Writer,* says that metaphor is a kind of instant poetry.[9] And poetry is an excellent place to find some of the best metaphors, because a poet expresses ideas by using the fewest words possible to make pictures that readers will recognize and relate to.

Colors will always seem a little different after reading about them in Mary O'Neill's *Hailstones and Halibut Bones.*

She speaks of purple,

*It's sort of a great
Grandmother to pink.*

And of pink

*Pink is the beautiful
Little sister of red*

And of orange,

*And in the fall
When the leaves are turning
Orange is the smell
Of a bonfire burning . . .*[10]

Nor will everyday objects seem the same after reading Beatrice Janosco's poem, "The Garden Hose," which begins "In the gray evening/ I see a long green serpent/ With its tail in the dahlias . . ."[11]

Fit your figures of speech to the characters and action and to the mood and setting of your story. A city setting could have someone slinking like an alley cat around trash cans, and a country story might have the character moving like a barn cat stalking a field mouse.

MIXED METAPHORS

Be careful about using too many comparisons. They not only lose their effectiveness but also get tangled up. After saying that Mary's lamb has fleece as white as snow, it would be confusing to add that the fleece kept the lamb as warm as toast.

CLICHÉS

Clichés are apt but time-worn expressions or ideas. Figures of speech that are used too often can become clichés. *White as snow* and *warm as toast* are clichés. If a metaphor or simile comes to you too quickly or easily, remember that it may well have come just as easily to hundreds of other people.

Clichés won't help a reader to see in a new way, but they can be useful. Take an old expression and make a new one out of it:

fleece as white as snow
fleece as soft as snow
snow as soft as wool
snow like woolly sweaters on all the bushes

MR. BROWNING'S RATS

Someone has said that words not only whisper and shout, they also leap and creep. To see what a master could do with words, read Robert Browning's "The Pied Piper of Hamelin."

> *Great rats, small rats, lean rats, brawny rats,*
> *Brown rats, black rats, gray rats, tawny rats,*
> *Grave old plodders, gay young friskers . . .*

He is describing the rats as they follow the piper. First, the slow-moving, elderly ones:

Grave old plodders

By the very construction of those words you cannot hurry them. Say them: *Grave old plodders.* The words take time to pronounce.

Then he goes on to the youthful rats:

gay young friskers

Like the young rats, those words skip along.

Edgar Allan Poe was another master of words. Hunt up his almost forgotten poem, "The Bells," to see what he could do with *onomatopoeia*—words imitating the sounds they represent, and alliteration—the repetition of sounds at the beginning of words or in accented syllables.

After seeing the pictures these two writers could make with words, start watching for word cousins, the relationship that special letters seem to have with certain families of words. Use these samples as starters for your own lists.

130

WORD COUSINS

B	D	J	Q
bang	dreary	joke	queasy
bark	drab	jovial	quake
bellow	dark	jolly	quail
brawl	dull	jest	qualm

SL	SN
sllther	snarl
slimy	snide
slippery	sneaky
sleazy	sniveling

Words with L-sounds give soft, quiet effects:

lullaby	sleepy
mellow	silent

The sounds of T, R, K (spelled with either K or C) can be harsh or hard:

choke	strike	shatter
crash	squawk	twist

The explosive sound of P often shows action:

chop	leap	plunge
clap	pop	whoop

Blow, winds, and crack your cheeks!
rage! blow!
You cataracts and hurricanes, spout . . .
　　　　　　　　　—William Shakespeare,
　　　　　　　　　　　　King Lear

"The question is," said Alice, "whether you can make words mean so many different things."

"The question is," said Humpty Dumpty, "which is to be master—that's all."

—Lewis Carroll,
Through the Looking Glass

SOME THINGS TO THINK ABOUT

The difference one word can make:

Joe rode his motorcycle *when* he had a job.
Joe rode his motorcycle *while* he had a job.
Joe rode his motorcycle *before* he had a job.
Joe rode his motorcycle *if* he had a job.
Joe rode his motorcycle *because* he had a job.

Be aware of the sound of the words you use as well as of their meaning. On the other hand, it isn't the wonderful words you use, it is the ideas and images that the words convey.

Good similes can light up a paragraph as a smile lights up a face.
Metaphors are the icing on the pound cake of ordinary prose.[12]

—James J. Kilpatrick,
The Writer's Art

TEN

REVISION—SEEING AGAIN

*The writer . . . must be his own best enemy.
He must accept the criticism of others and be
suspicious of it; he must accept the praise of
others and be even more suspicious of it. . . .*[1]
—Donald M. Murray,
"The Maker's Eye"

SEEING AGAIN

You've written the final word of your story—but you are not finished. Now comes the step called revision. Re-vision. Seeing again. Looking at your story another time. Phyllis A. Whitney says that good books aren't written; they are rewritten. "Revision is a key phase of your novel writing."[2] This is just as true in writing plays, articles, poems, and short stories.

Some writers maintain that they do no rewriting. Those who say this can be one of three types:

- The would-be writers who believe they cannot do better because their ability is so poor.
- The would-be writers who believe they cannot do better because their work is so good.
- The experienced professionals who are able to create any necessary number of mental drafts before they begin their actual writing.

There are very few of the third type of writers.

In response to questions about rewriting, professionals are more likely to say, as does Sidney Sheldon, "I do up to a dozen complete rewrites before my publisher ever sees a manuscript."[3] In an interview, Anthony Burgess said, "I might revise a page twenty times."[4] Frank O'Connor, when asked, "Do you rewrite?" answered, "Endlessly, endlessly, endlessly." And Dorothy Parker once told an interviewer, "I can't write five words but that I change seven."[5]

INSPIRATION IS JUST THE BEGINNING

Experienced writers consider revision the place the real writing begins, that it is not a matter of going back, but, rather, the time of going forward into a new phase of creativity.

Revision is not to be confused with proofreading or copying over. Nor is it to be confused with the changing, taking out, and putting in that happens in the writing of a first draft. Revision is looking at that first draft again. It is the opportunity to make what is less than good, good, and what is good, better.

IT TAKES TIME TO BE OBJECTIVE

The first thing to do in the process of revision is to do nothing. Nothing, that is, but to put your manuscript on the shelf, in a drawer, out of sight, for a resting period. That period should be at least overnight, better yet, several days or weeks or even longer. Gabriel Garcia Marquez, Nobel Prize–winning author, is quoted as saying he puts a manuscript to sleep in a drawer for a year. "A certain distance has to develop so that I can read it objectively. . . . It allows me to be the editor."[6]

After a time for distancing and when you are ready to work on your story again, first read it straight through. See it with new eyes. Or, better yet, hear your story. Have someone read it to you. Tape it and play it back. Read it out loud to yourself. The ear catches what the eye slides over.

INSPECTION TIME

If we wished to return briefly to the house-building analogy, this would be the time for the building inspector to appear with his clipboard and questions.

As you go through your manuscript for the first time after its rest period, listen. Listen to how your story sounds.

- Does the writing have cadence?
- Are the sentences easy to read? Have some word combinations become tongue twisters?
- Are sentence endings strong, or do some sentences ramble or fade away?
- Does dialogue sound natural? Is each character speaking in an individual voice?
- Does the story move along smoothly?
- Is the viewpoint choice right? Would the story be stronger if presented from the viewpoint of another character?
- Is the style of telling, such as humorous, serious, or mysterious, the best for this story?

IS THE CONSTRUCTION SOUND?

Now let's look at the story's structure.

- Does the story begin at the right place?
- Does the beginning introduce characters, situation, and setting?
- Do the story scenes have conflict? Do they create new problems for the main character?
- Do events happen in believable, logical order?
- Are there weak places in the story?
- Have you told too much? Not enough? Have you given away important information too soon?
- Does the story stay with the viewpoint you've chosen? If you tell the story from more than one viewpoint, are the shifts clear?
- Are any important details left out? (What about Grandma and Rover?)
- Are there beautiful sentences that add nothing but words to the story?
- Does the story have a believable, logical, satisfying ending?

Writing so your reader understands is not enough. Write so your reader does not misunderstand. Remember, reader and writer are not working together. You, the writer, have to catch and hold the readers' attention and give them information and entertainment worth their time and effort.

WHAT HAVE YOU SAID?

As you read or listen, you will discover what you actually wrote. Is it what you thought you were writing? Look upon your first draft as an exploration of your ideas. Have you said what you wanted to say? Have you created the feeling you wanted?

Think carefully about any questions that come to mind as you read for a second or third time.

- Do title and beginning still fit your story?
- Is there enough showing, enough telling?
- Do you find patterns you hadn't realized were there?

These might be unwanted patterns such as too many adverbs or adjectives or favorite words. (I didn't realize I'd used *very* five times on that page. I probably shouldn't have used *very* at all.)

Or you might find good patterns of ideas, symbols, or images. Do they give your story a deeper or a different meaning? Should they be developed?

- Have you put emotion into the story, not your emotion but the character's emotion? Will it become the reader's emotion? "If you would write emotionally," says James J. Kilpatrick, "be first unemotional. If you would move your readers to tears, do not let them see you cry."[7]
- And last, have you given your reader something to think about after the story ends?

DETAILS

Now is the time to check your details again. Did Shakespeare say that, or was it Mark Twain? When did Gwendolyn's name change to Emmeline? Are there any dangling phrases or orphaned pronouns? Does "She gave him a big smack" mean she slapped him or she kissed him? Is *everybody* singular or plural? Is that word a noun or a verb? Remember, fruit flies like bananas but time flies like the wind.

Correct grammar is important, but a preposition can come at the end of a sentence, and an infinitive can, on occasion, be split quite effectively. Careful but natural use of words and grammar will make smooth writing and easy understanding.

A PINCH OF PUNCTUATION

Never underestimate the power of a comma—or a hyphen or a question mark.

"What a party!"
"What? A party?"

I have twenty five dollar bills.
How many?
I have twenty five-dollar bills.
I have twenty-five dollar bills.
I do not have any twenty-five-dollar bills.

We use commas more than we use any other punctuation marks, and they give us more trouble than any other punctuation marks. They can change meanings and they can save or cause confusion.

That's a pretty small house.
(That house is quite small.)
That's a pretty, small house.
(That's an attractive small house.)

There is much disagreement about the necessity of the comma known as the serial comma. In a series, this comma goes just before the conjunction:

first, second, and third
Tom, Dick, and Harry

The comma before *and* is the serial comma.

If you plan to omit serial commas, be sure your sentence says what you want it to say.

> *He called, "Tom, Dick and Harry are leaving now."*

Without the serial comma, he seems to be saying, "Come on, Tom, and tell Dick and Harry good-bye."

> *He called, "Tom, Dick, and Harry are leaving now."*

With the serial comma, we understand that he means, "There go the three of them."

> *When I saw our house, my mother hanging the wash and good old Rover, I knew I was glad to be home again.*
> *When I saw our house, my mother hanging the wash, and good old Rover, I knew I was glad to be home again.*

An editor once said that the three most important reasons for punctuation are clarity, clarity, and clarity. Use the common, everyday punctuation marks—commas, periods, quotation marks, apostrophes, and question marks—to make your meaning clear. Look over your manuscript to see if any punctuation needs to be added or if unnecessary punctuation needs to be taken out. Watch, especially, for dashes (—), ellipses (. . .), exclamation points (! and never !!), or quotation marks around cute little words or phrases. About these devices, best advice is, "Consider them like garlic and use accordingly."

KNOW WHEN TO STOP

A seventeenth-century poet, Nicolas Boileau-Despréaux, gave encouragement with these words to remember as you revise: "Hasten slowly without losing heart."

But remember also the words that a Roman author, Pliny the Younger, wrote hundreds of years earlier: "Too much polishing weakens rather than improves a work."

Do the best work you can and stop. Copy this final draft, and then, to make it ready for the next reader—friend, classmate, teacher, and perhaps one day an editor—do one more meticulous job of searching for typos, misspellings, or any other mistakes. Reading your manuscript will be an editor's job, but proofreading your manuscript is not.

A FINAL WORD

We began, in the introduction, by saying that writing is communication. Now we end by saying it again. It is moving your thoughts to your readers. You want your ideas to reach others in accurate, understandable, and compelling form. Ways of doing that, shown in the preceding chapters, are not the only ways, but they are ones that have proved successful for many writers.

Some of the stories you write may closely follow the story-plan equation. In others, you may want to experiment with new ways of telling, with different ways of showing, with unusual ways of writing. Study what has worked for other writers, then find out and do whatever works best for your writing and for you. And keep in mind this bit of counsel attributed to Friedrich Nietzsche,

> *This is my way . . .*
> *What is your way?*
> The *way doesn't exist.*[8]

APPENDIX: THE WRITER'S NOTEBOOK

"The horror of that moment," the King went on, "I shall never, never forget!"
"You will, though," the Queen said, "if you don't make a memorandum of it."
—Lewis Carroll,
Through the Looking Glass

Every writer should keep a notebook. Call it what you will—notebook, journal, log, diary, commonplace book, scrapbook—or shoe box. Have a place to keep clippings, quotes, ideas, interesting words, story plans, titles (and authors) of books you've read, titles of books you're going to read.

The Russian artist Marc Chagall said, "Even when I'm not working I'm working." Writers are always working. Notebooks are for keeping records of that work.

A writer is an observer, people watcher, eavesdropper. You will not merely look, you will see; you will not just hear, you will listen. And you will make notes, even if, like the White King, you are sure you'll never, *never* forget.

Reading is another way you work when you're not working. A few professional writers maintain that they are too busy writing to have time to read. Far more say *If you would write, read.* James J. Kilpatrick calls libraries the lumberyards where writers go for building supplies.

Read everything you can. If you want to write short stories, read short stories. But read longer fiction and nonfiction, too. Read poetry. And read books you'll find on the shelves in the children's library. Many of them could be, should be, on the adult shelves as well.

Read Gillian Paton Walsh's *Hengest's Tale.* Read *Badger's Parting Gifts* by Susan Varley. Read from the books that pleased you as a child. Do they please you still? Read from the poetry collections and read the picture books. Picture books, like poetry, must express their ideas in the fewest possible words, so they both speak and make pictures with metaphor.

Make notes of phrases, sentences, whole paragraphs that catch your interest. Put them in your notebook (documented, of course) to go back to, to read again.

Read for variety. If nothing more, read a few lines here and a few lines there, from the very old, the not-so-old, and the new.

> *. . . came through the wan night slithering the shadowthing . . .*
>
> —*Beowulf*

> *I heard a voice that cried "Balder the beautiful is dead—is dead—*
>
> —*Esaias Tegner,*
> *Drapa*

When the brig Orion, three weeks out from Havana, appeared off her home port of New Bethany, Maine, Miss Evangeline Frye was just parting her bed curtains, formally banishing night.

—Paul Fleischman,
"The Binnacle Boy,"
Graven Images

A writer also has to have time to think and to wonder. Give yourself that time. Wondering is the beginning of all creative acts. Every building and bridge, every pen and pencil, and yes, every book, began as a dream and a visualization. Take time to dream and think. Then give shape to your thoughts by putting them into words and onto paper to save, in your notebook, into your shoe box, so that you can go back to them to read and to read again.

And so you'll take time to look, to think, to wonder. You'll read—for enjoyment, yes, but also to find out what others say and how they say it. You'll read to discover what you want to write and what you don't want to write.

Just don't read to keep from writing. Why? The Greek philosopher Epictetus said it best: "If you wish to be a good writer, write."

SOURCE NOTES

INTRODUCTION

1.Phyllis A. Whitney, *Guide to Fiction Writing*. Boston: The Writer, Inc., 1983, p. ix.

CHAPTER ONE

1.Robert Newton Peck, *Secrets of Successful Fiction*. Cincinnati: Writer's Digest Books, 1980, Chapter 4.

2.Roger von Oech, *A Whack on the Side of the Head*. New York: Warner Books, 1983, p. 7.

3.Marjorie Holmes, *Writing Articles from the Heart*. Cincinnati: Writer's Digest Books, 1993, p. 15.

CHAPTER TWO

1.Fannie Flagg, *Fried Green Tomatoes at the Whistle Stop Cafe*. New York: McGraw-Hill, Inc., paperback edition, 1988, p. 40.

2.Tobias Wolff, *This Boy's Life*. New York: Harper & Row Publishers, Perennial Library Edition, 1980, p. 8.

3.Jane Fitz-Randolph, *How to Write for Children & Young Adults*. Boulder, Colorado: Johnson Books, Revised Edition, 1987, p. 89.

CHAPTER FOUR

1.Joan Aiken, *The Wolves of Willoughby Chase*. Garden City, New York: Doubleday & Company, Inc., 1962, p. 7.

2.Aileen Fisher, "Zero Weather," *Runny Days, Sunny Days*. London & New York: Abelard-Schuman Ltd., 1958, p. 111.

3.Annie Dillard, *Holy the Firm*. New York: Harper & Row Publishers, 1977, p. 73.

4.Jane Langton, *The Transcendental Murders*. New York: Harper & Row Publishers, 1964, p. 139.

5.Kathleen C. Phillips, *Sounds in the Dark of the Night*. (Work in progress.)

6.Kathleen C. Phillips, *Katie McCrary and the Wiggins Crusade*. New York: Elsevier/Nelson Books, 1980, p. 78.

7.*Ibid.*, 119.

8.John Lutz, "Setting for Suspense," *The Writer*, July 1974, Vol. 87, No. 7, pp. 21–23.

9.Lesley Conger, "The Magic of Pictures, The Magic of Words," *The Writer*, July 1975, Vol. 88, No. 7, pp. 7–8.

CHAPTER FIVE

1.Barnaby Conrad, *The Complete Guide to Writing Fiction*. Cincinnati: Writer's Digest Books, 1990, p. 247.

2.Jane Fitz-Randolph, *How to Write for Children & Young Adults*, p. 28.

3.Jerome Stern, *Making Shapely Fiction*. New York: W.W. Norton & Company, 1991, p. 216.

4.Jane Fitz-Randolph, *How to Write for Children & Young Adults*, pp, 55–56.

5.Rudyard Kipling, "The Cat That Walked By Himself," *Just So Stories*. New York: Henry Holt and Company, 1987, p. 78.

6.Mike Royko, column, Chicago *Tribune*, reprinted in Boulder (Colorado) *Daily Camera*, November 30, 1980.

7.Robert Newton Peck, *A Day No Pigs Would Die*. New York: Dell Publishing Co., Inc., 1982, p. 7.

8.P. J. Petersen, *Good-bye to Good Ol' Charlie*. Dell Publishing Co., Inc., 1987, p. 3.

9.Ronald B. Tobias, *Theme & Strategy*. Cincinnati: Writer's Digest Books, 1989, p. 127.

10.*Ibid.*, 97

11.Barnaby Conrad, *The Complete Guide to Writing Fiction*, pp. 10 & 111.

12.Lajos Egri, *The Art of Dramatic Writing*. New York: Simon and Schuster, 1960, p. 2.

13.Leonard Bishop, *Dare to Be a Great Writer*. Cincinnati: Writer's Digest Books, 1988, p. 311.

CHAPTER SIX

1.Milo O. Frank, *How to Get Your Point Across in 30 Seconds—Or Less*. New York: Simon and Schuster, 1986, p. 15.

2.Phyllis A. Whitney, *Guide to Fiction Writing*, p. 50.

3.John Fischer, "A Small Buried Treasure," *The Edge of the Chair*, Joan Kahn, ed. New York: Harper & Row Publishers, Inc., 1967, p. 509.

4.Ken Follett, *The Pillars of the Earth*. New York: William Morrow and Company, Inc., 1989, p. 11.

5.John Gardner, *Nickel Mountain*. New York: Alfred A. Knopf, 1973, p. 3.

6.E. B. White, *Stuart Little*. New York: Harper & Row Publishers, Inc., 1945, p. 1.

7.Lloyd Alexander, *The Cat Who Wished to Be a Man*. New York: E.P. Dutton & Co., Inc., 1973, p. 1.

8.Mary Peace, *Fireflies*. Lakemount, Georgia: Copple House Books, Inc., 1986, p. 5.

9.George Orwell, *1984*. New York: New American Library, 1983, p. 5.

10.Jerry Earl Brown, *Under the City of Angels*. New York: Bantam Books, Inc., 1981, p. 5.

11.Robert Olen Butler, "The Trip Back," *A Good Scent from a Strange Mountain*. New York: Penguin Books, 1992, p. 29.

12.Clive Barker, "Dread," *The Dark Descent*, David G. Harwell, ed. New York: Tor, 1987, p. 339.

13.Charles Dickens, *A Christmas Carol*. New York: Pocket Books, 1958, p. 11.

14.Daphne du Maurier, *Rebecca*. New York: Doubleday & Company, Inc., 1938; Avon Books, 1971, p. 1.

15.Ray Bradbury, "Pillar of Fire," *The Other Side of the Moon*, August Derleth, ed. New York: Pellegrini & Cudahy, 1949, p. 212.

16.David Ordan, "Any Minute Mom Should Come Blasting Through the Door," *Sudden Fiction*, Robert Shapard, and James Thomas, eds. Layton, Utah: Gibbs Smith, Publisher, A Peregrine Smith Book, 1986, p. 196.

17.Ken Follett, *The Key to Rebecca*. New York: William Morrow and Company, Inc., 1980, p. 15.

18.Georgianne Ensign, *Great Beginnings*. New York: HarperCollins Publishers, 1993, p. 197.

CHAPTER SEVEN

1.Dwight V. Swain, "High Middle," *The Writer's Digest Handbook of Short Story Writing*, Volume II,

Jean M. Fredette, ed. Cincinnati: Writer's Digest Books, 1988, p. 96.

2.Cecelia Holland, *Great Maria*. New York: Alfred A. Knopf, 1974, p. 5.

3.Joan Aiken, *The Way to Write for Children*. New York: St. Martin's Press, 1982, p. 52.

4.Robert Newton Peck, *Secrets of Successful Fiction*, Chapter 3.

CHAPTER EIGHT

1.Lawrence Block, *Writing the Novel: From Plot to Print*. Cincinnati: Writer's Digest Books, 1979, pp. 145–6.

2.Douglas Adams, *The Long Dark Tea-time of the Soul*. New York: Pocket Books, Simon and Schuster, Inc., 1978, pp. 162–3.

CHAPTER NINE

1.Paul Fleischman, "The Man of Influence," *Graven Images*. New York: Harper & Row Publishers, 1982, p. 63.

2.James J. Kilpatrick, *The Writer's Art*. Kansas City: Andrews, McMeel & Parker, 1984, pp. 106–107.

3.Kathleen C. Phillips and Barbara Steiner, *Catching Ideas*. Englewood, Colorado: Teacher Ideas Press, Libraries Unlimited, Inc., 1988, p. 45.

4.Theodore Taylor, *The Cay*. New York: Doubleday & Company, Inc., 1969, p. 9.

5.Sid Fleischman, *Jingo Django*. Boston: Little, Brown & Co., 1971, p. 3.

6.William Mayne, *Sand*. New York: E.P. Dutton & Company, Inc., 1965, p. 7.

7.Alix Ainsley, *The House of Whispering Aspens*. New York: Zebra Books, 1985, p. 280.

8.Frank Bonham, *Mystery of the Fat Cat.* New York: E.P. Dutton & Company, Inc., 1968, pp. 16 & 22.

9.Theodore M. Bernstein, *The Careful Writer.* New York: Atheneum, 1973, p. 275.

10.Mary O'Neill, *Hailstones and Halibut Bones.* New York: Doubleday, 1989, unpaged.

11.Beatrice Janosco, "The Garden Hose," *Reflections on a Gift of Watermelon Pickle*, Stephen Dunning et al., eds. New York: Lothrop, Lee & Shepard, 1967, p. 110.

12.Kilpatrick, p. 97.

CHAPTER TEN

1.Donald M. Murray, "The Maker's Eye: Revising Your Own Manuscript," *The Writer*, October 1973, Vol. 86, No. 10, p. 14.

2.Phyllis A. Whitney, *Guide to Fiction Writing*, p. 124.

3.Sidney Sheldon, "The Professional Response," *The Writer*, December 1993, Vol. 106, No. 12, p. 10.

4.Anthony Burgess, quoted by Donald M. Murray, "The Maker's Eye," *The Writer*, October 1973, p. 15.

5.Frank O'Connor and Dorothy Parker, quoted by Malcolm Cowley, ed., *Writers at Work.* New York: The Viking Press, 1958, pp. 10 & 168.

6.Gabriel Garcia Marquez, "Roving Editor," The Writer, September 1974, Vol. 87, No. 9, p. 6.

7.James J. Kilpatrick, *The Writer's Art*, p. 125.

8.Friedrich Nietzche, quoted by Wayne W. Dwyer, *Pulling Your Own Strings.* New York: Thomas Y. Crowell Co., 1978, pp. 208–9.

FOR FURTHER READING

THE CREATIVE PROCESS

Downey, Bill. *Right Brain . . . Write On! Overcoming Writer's Block and Achieving Your Creative Potential.* Englewood Cliffs, N.J.: Prentice-Hall, Inc., 1984.

Golman, Daniel, et al. *The Creative Spirit.* Companion to the PBS Television Series. New York: E.P. Dutton, 1992.

Rico, Gabriele Lusser. *Writing the Natural Way. Using Right-brain Techniques to Release Your Expressive Powers.* Los Angeles: J.P. Tarcher, 1983.

von Oech, Roger. *A Whack on the Side of the Head. How to Unlock Your Mind for Innovation.* New York: Warner Books, 1983.

BOOKS ABOUT WRITING

Asher, Sandy. *Wild Words! How to Train Them to Tell Stories.* New York: Walker and Co., 1989.

Bauer, Marion Dane. *What's Your Story? A Young*

Person's Guide to Writing Fiction. Boston: Clarion Books, 1992.

Brande, Dorothea. *Becoming a Writer.* Los Angeles: J.P. Tarcher, 1981.

Burnett, Hallie. *On Writing the Short Story.* New York: Harper and Row, 1983.

Conrad, Barnaby. *The Complete Guide to Writing Fiction.* Cincinnati: Writer's Digest Books, 1990.

Fredette, Jean M., ed. *The Writer's Digest Handbook of Short Story Writing,* Volume II. Cincinnati: Writer's Digest Books, 1988.

Fitz-Randolph, Jane. *How to Write for Children & Young Adults.* Boulder, Colo.: Johnson Books, 1987.

Giblin, James Cross. *Writing Books for Young People.* Boston: The Writer, Inc., 1990.

Kilpatrick, James J. *The Writer's Art.* Kansas City, Mo.: Andrew, McMeel & Parker, 1984.

Maugham, W. Somerset. *A Writer's Notebook.* New York: Penguin, 1984.

Meredith, Robert C., and John D. Fitzgerald. *Structuring Your Novel.* New York: HarperCollins, 1993.

Norton, James H., and Francis Gretton. *Writing Incredibly Short Plays, Poems, and Stories.* New York: Harcourt Brace Jovanovich, Inc., 1972.

Peck, Robert Newton. *Fiction Is Folks. How to Create Unforgettable Characters.* Cincinnati: Writer's Digest Books, 1983.

————. *Secrets of Successful Fiction.* Cincinnati: Writer's Digest Books, 1980.

Reed, Kit. *Revision.* Cincinnati: *Writer's Digest Books,* 1989.

Stanley, George Edward. *Writing Short Stories for Young People.* Cincinnati: Writer's Digest Books, 1986.

Stern, Jerome. *Making Shapely Fiction.* New York: W.W. Norton & Co., 1991.

Tchudi, Susan and Stephen. *The Young Writer's Handbook. A practical guide for the beginner who is serious about writing*. New York: Macmillan Publishing Co., 1987.

Whitney, Phyllis A. *Guide to Fiction Writing*. Boston: The Writer, Inc., 1982.

Williamson, J.N., ed. *How to Write Tales of Horror, Fantasy and Science Fiction*. Cincinnati: Writer's Digest Books, 1987.

INSPIRATION AND IDEAS: FICTION AND NONFICTION, POETRY AND PROSE

Dunning, Stephen, et al. *Reflections on a Gift of Watermelon Pickle. . . and Other Modern Verse*. New York: Lothrop, Lee & Shepard, 1967.

———. *Some Haystacks Don't Even Have Any Needle*. Glenview, Ill.: Scott, Foresman & Co., 1969.

Ensign, Georgianne. *Great Beginnings. Opening Lines of Great Novels*. New York: HarperCollins, 1993.

Fleischman, Paul. *Graven Images*. New York: Harper and Row, 1982.

———. *Joyful Noise: Poems for Two Voices*. New York: Harper and Row, 1988.

Livingston, Myra Cohn. *Poem-making*. New York: HarperCollins, 1991.

McKay, David, ed. *A Flock of Words*. New York: Harcourt, Brace and World, Inc., 1969.

Merriam, Eve. *Out Loud*. New York: Atheneum, 1973.

———. *A Word or Two with You*. New York: Atheneum, 1981.

O'Neill, Mary. *Hailstones and Halibut Bones*. New York: Doubleday, 1989.

———. *Words, Words, Words*. Garden City, N.Y.: Doubleday, 1966.

Phillips, Kathleen C., and Barbara Steiner. *Catching Ideas*. Englewood, Colo.: Teacher Ideas Press, Libraries Unlimited, Inc., 1988.

Steiner, Barbara, and Kathleen C. Phillips. *Journal Keeping with Young People*. Englewood, Colo.: Teacher Ideas Press, Libraries Unlimited, Inc., 1991.

Also, short story collections such as The Pushcart Prize books (best stories from small presses) Pushcart Press, Wainscott, New York; and Delacorte Press books edited by Donald R. Gallo, including *Sixteen; Visions; Short Circuits*; and *Connections*.

REFERENCE, TECHNIQUE, AND STYLE

Bernstein, Theodore M. *The Careful Writer. A Modern Guide to English Usage*. New York: Atheneum, 1965.

Boston, Bruce O., ed. *STET! Tricks of the Trade for Writers and Editors*. Alexandria, Va.: Editorial Experts, Inc., 1986.

Cook, Claire K. *Line by Line. How to Improve Your Own Writing*. Boston: Houghton, Mifflin Co., 1985.

Gordon, Karen Elizabeth. *The Transitive Vampire. A Handbook of Grammar for the Innocent, the Eager, and the Doomed*. New York: Times Books, 1984.

———. *The New Well-Tempered Sentence. A Punctuation Handbook for the Innocent, the Eager, and the Doomed*. New York: Ticknor and Fields, 1993.

Rodale, J.I. *The Synonym Finder*. Emmaus, Pa.: Rodale Press, 1978.

INDEX

ABOUT THE AUTHOR

Kathleen C. Phillips has co-authored *Catching Ideas* with Barbara Steiner, and has written the novels *Sounds in the Dark of the Night* and *Katie McCrary and the Wiggins Crusade*. She lives in Boulder, Colorado.